KNOWLEDGE IS THE New gold

HOW TO TURN YOUR KNOWLEDGE INTO AN ONLINE COURSE THAT MAKES MONEY AND IMPACT LIVES

STEPHANIE OBI

Published by ST HUB LIMITED
www.stephanieobi.com
info@stephanieobi.com
www.instagram.com/stephobi

ISBN: 978-198-306-373-2

Cover Design: *Ida Fia Sveningsson*
Photography: *Gazmadu Studios*
Book Layout Design: *Weedo Creative Coy*

Dedication

I dedicate this book to my family,
Mr Samuel Obi, Mrs Mayen Obi,
Genevieve Obi, Princess Obi, and Obi Samuel
You are the wind beneath my wings.

FREE GIFT!

To say thank you for buying my book,
I would like to give you a free gift!

Content

Introduction

Anytime I read the story of the widow with the jar of oil in the bible, I always wondered what she really wanted Elisha to do for her.

She said to him, "My husband who served you is dead, and you know how he feared the Lord. But now, a creditor has come, threatening to take my two sons as slaves".

I guess she was expecting Elisha to give her some money to pay off her creditors or to give her a loan.

Instead, Elisha asked her a surprising question.

"Tell me, what do you have in the house?"

"Nothing at all, she replied, except a flask of oil."

She replied the way a lot of us typically reply when asked what we have.

We don't realise that we have something within us that can be created into products and sold.

We all have a skill, an experience, a gift that can be created into a product.

Like the widow, we look at our flask of oil helplessly and think that nothing can come out of it.

Elisha said to her, "Borrow as many empty jars as you can from your friends and neighbours, and then go into your house with your sons and shut the door behind you.

Pour the olive oil from your flask into the jars, setting each one aside when it is filled."

She did as she was told until all the jars were filled to the brim.

Then Elisha said to her, "Now sell your jars of olive oil, pay your debts, and you and your sons can live on what is left over".

Her problem was solved by using what she had to create a product and then selling it.

This is exactly what this book is about.

---

*God wants to supply all your needs,
using what you already have.*

You can turn the knowledge you already have into a product and sell it online.

In this book, I will be sharing with you how you can do this through online courses.

God wants to supply all your needs, using what you already have.

How I Discovered Online Courses

I was not in debt like the widow I just wrote about, but I experienced a different type of challenge that led me to discover online courses.

In my twenties, I faced a crisis.

On the outside, my life seemed perfect.

I was working in a multinational company and my future in the company seemed bright.

But on the inside, I was torn.

I was very unhappy.

I would break down and cry at the slightest things.

I felt as if I was wasting my life.

I was never excited to jump out of bed in the mornings.

I was not inspired by the work that I did.

It was just work.

I knew that I wanted to change my life, but I was not sure of where to start from.

'At some point, I had to ask myself this defining question:

"What do you have?"

At the time, I had a little hobby I used to do for fun.

I would make fashion accessories made out of a very popular African print fabric called Ankara and sell them to my friends.

I had been making accessories all through my days in the university, throughout the one year National Youth Service Corps programme (NYSC), all through my time in the corporate world and throughout my full-time MBA programme.

My hobby had by this time turned into a side business that used to bring me income.

So, I decided to show other ladies how to start a side business, focused on making and selling Ankara Accessories so that they too could become empowered.

I became so obsessed with the idea of helping other women start their own Ankara Accessories businesses and I went all out.

I designed my curriculum.

I designed starter kits for them.

I created fliers and marketed the workshop the best way I knew to.

However, this workshop was a disaster because nobody paid for it.
The sadness I felt from this forced me to start learning how to market effectively online. The next time I organised the workshop, I had four students sign up to attend.

I was overjoyed.

'We held the workshop in the garage of my parents' home. Throughout the entire day, I had such a burst of energy. I was so excited about what I was doing that I even forgot to eat.

As I recounted the experience to my friends, I kept saying, "This is what I want to do with my life."

I was so happy, and when I think about that day, I believe I was even happier than the ladies who attended the workshop.

I felt so fulfilled knowing that I was actually making a difference in someone else's life.

I continued marketing my workshops online and then I started getting messages from people all over the country.

"I live in Onitsha, can you come to my city to organise a workshop?"

"I live in Yola and it would be too expensive for me to travel to Lagos. Please is there any chance that you would be coming this way?"

I could not travel to all the cities where I was getting requests from because I was still working at my 9 to 5 at the time, and so I decided to do something else instead.

I decided to create an online course.

With an online course, I could just record training videos, upload them on a website and give people access.

I wouldn't have to travel, and my clients would be able to access the trainings irrespective of where they lived.
They also wouldn't have to pay additional costs such as transportation, accommodation, and so on. It looked like a win-win to me!

I got to work and on the 12th of September 2013, I launched my first online course.

Even though this was an act of faith and I believed for the best, I was still so surprised when people started paying for my online course.

I was surprised that people would pay for my course even though they had never met me in real life. They were ready to buy from me even though I was not a known brand or a celebrity.

I was surprised that people would pay to watch video content online and to buy data to watch these videos. This was in 2013 by the way and access to the internet was expensive.

I felt like I had stumbled on a secret.

You mean, I can teach what I know and people will really pay me from all over the world?

Today, this course has been taken by ladies in over nine countries.

One particular month, the sales I made from this online course matched my monthly salary in paid employment.

I screamed out loud, "I'm not even doing this full time, what will happen if I were doing this full time?"

As if the money I was making from the course was not enough, I started getting thank you messages from ladies who had taken the course.

One of them wrote to me, and said:

"Stephanie, when I stumbled on you online, I was in a bad place. I just came out of a very bad relationship. My self esteem was gone. I didn't believe in myself. I saw you smiling and talking about how I could start an Ankara accessories business to empower myself.

I decided to take one of your online courses and this turned out to be a great decision. I have started my own Ankara accessories business. I am making my own money. I now believe in myself.

I just want to say thank you for changing my life."

At first, I did not understand how Ankara accessories could have such a huge impact in people's lives ...yes, I knew it would help them make an extra stream of income, but I did not realise that money was only a small part of the transformation they were going through.

I kept getting these type of emails from my clients, and then it really dawned on me that I had stumbled on a way of making money and impacting lives.

The best part was, I was using the knowledge I already had, that could have been lying fallow.

As of today, I have launched over twenty online courses and over 600 people have taken my online courses from over nine countries.

I have also helped lots of people to launch their own online courses and my clients have gotten great results with their own courses.

I wrote this book because I want to help you to discover your own jar of oil and turn it into an online course so that you can become financially free.

Apart from making money, online courses have helped me to:
- Become joyful and fulfilled
- Leave my 9 - 5 to focus on doing what I'm passionate about
- Help so many people in different countries to get amazing results
- Work from anywhere I want
- Live a flexible lifestyle
- Speak at national and international conferences
- Travel when and where I want
- Become known as an expert in my field

I also want to help you to step into your purpose. Most people who have been called to impact lives struggle with fears that hold them back for so long.

It's time to answer the call.

I've broken down the book into three major parts:

Part 1: The Big Deal about Online Courses
Here, we're going to lay the foundation of what an online course really is and what it's not, why it's such a big opportunity and how much money you can earn from online courses.

Part 2: Crush your Mindset Blocks
I will address some of the fears and limiting beliefs that might be stopping you from taking advantage of the opportunities in online courses, so that you can confidently launch your own course.

Part 3: The Course Launched Delivered Method
I will share with you my signature method on how to successfully launch and deliver your online course. One of the most painful discoveries which new course creators experience is that they create online courses and

nobody pays for them. This has happened to me before and after launching over 20 online courses, I now have a proven system of launching online courses that make money. Another challenge new course creators face is that they create courses that don't help their students achieve results. If you follow the Course Launched Delivered Method, your students will scream your name from the rooftops and pray for you consistently for changing their lives.

My prayer is that this book changes your life and the lives of the people you have been sent to impact.

The best time to start is now.

How to Use This Book

I'll recommend that you read this book sequentially first, before focusing on the areas you really need help with.

This is because each concept builds up on the previous, and you may miss out a vital step.

As you read this book, you will find the following sections across the chapters:

1. **Success Stories**

   To inspire you as you read this book, I will share several success stories of people just like you who committed to the Course Launched Delivered method and launched their online courses.

2. **Exercises**

   To help you implement the lessons, I will also share exercises for you to work on across the different chapters in the book.

3. **Reflections**

   In a lot of ways, turning your knowledge into an online course that will impact lives is an assignment that might have been laid in your heart. One thing that is common among people who have this urge in their heart to impact lives, is that they always resist the call upon their lives.

As I was writing this book, I reflected on another person in the Bible who was also called to complete an assignment and who tried to resist it. Moses. I fondly call him "The Reluctant Messenger". In the Reflections sections in the book, I'll share with you how Moses overcame his reluctance, so that you too can overcome yours.

- Stephanie Obi

PART 1

The Big Deal About Online Courses

There are many ways to make money from the knowledge you already have.

You can:

- Write a book
- Record an audio CD
- Accept paid speaking engagements
- Coach individuals
- Consult for companies
- Host a live workshop
- Create sponsored content for brands
- Create online courses

In this book, we focus on online courses because it seems like it's still a huge secret.

An article on www.inc.com described online education as a $107 billion industry that nobody is talking about.

If you are paying some attention, you will notice that all the most of the successful thought leaders have online courses.

Even celebrities are now creating online courses.

They are using online courses to reach out to thousands of people all over the world, who would ordinarily not easily have access to them.

Just think about it: Someone creates one online course. Hundreds to thousands of people pay for it from all over the world. She keeps reselling that same online course, and doesn't even need an office, warehouse or publisher to launch the course.

Now, more than ever, people are trying to achieve their life goals and are looking for anyone who has results to teach them how to get results too.

The best part is, if you have the results they are looking for, you too can create your own online course.

THE BIG DEAL ABOUT ONLINE COURSES

Anytime I tell people that I create and sell online courses, I always watch to see the expressions on their faces.

Some frown and others squint their eyes as they try to understand what I am saying.

"Online course, online course…interesting…What exactly is an online course? Is it like Coursera or what?"

I would see their eyes glaze over as I tried to explain this concept they had never seen to them.

At a point in my career, I actually used to be frustrated that people did not really understand what I was doing…but with time, I got better at explaining what an online course really is.

First things first, an online course is a training program that is delivered online, so that people can access the training irrespective of where they live. They don't have to travel to a particular location to access the training program, and they can watch it from the comfort of their homes or while they are in a moving vehicle as long as they have a device that has access to the internet. They can also watch the training from their smartphone, tablet or laptop.

How Does it Work?

An online course consists of pre-recorded lessons which could be in video, audio or text format. They are usually arranged sequentially in an easy-to-follow manner, so that anybody taking the course can easily understand what is being taught.

The lessons are also delivered through an online school, which learners access using a unique username and password that they receive after paying for the course. The students can log in at any time of the day to watch the lessons.

Types of Online Courses

There are two major types of online courses: mini courses and transformational courses.

Mini courses focus on helping students learn a skill or make slight improvements. They usually consist of only lessons, PDF workbooks and resource guides as the participants would be expected to go through the lessons on their own.

Transformational courses, on the other hand, focus on helping the students to go through a complete transformation. Every step of the way, they need some form of additional support and mentoring from the course creator. In addition to the lessons, workbooks and resource guides, the course creator would be expected to be available to answer questions and give feedback.

How Long Do Online Courses Last For?

The length of time it will take your student to go through your online course is usually dependent on what type of online course it is.

Mini courses are not complicated and the lessons can be consumed in a short period. Transformational courses take more time because it takes a while to get people to change. A good one should last for 60 - 90 days.

Anything longer than 90 days is usually too long, as your students might get tired or lose interest.

Why Do People Pay for Online Courses When There is Google?

Google is undoubtedly one of the best things that happened in our lifetime, but it is only a search engine. It curates information. Anytime you search for a phrase, it gives you too much information, and many times, people don't know where to start from or which of the information is relevant.

In the fast paced society we live in, a lot of people are looking for exact systems and formulas that can help them get the results they desperately need.

They don't have the time to search through all the information they find on Google, testing them out one after the other, to see which will work and which ones won't.

They are looking for exact results and a proven system to help them get those results. This is what online courses offer.

Why Would People Pay for Online Courses When There are Traditional Training Programmes?

Traditional training programmes are physical trainings like seminars, live workshops and so on.

They have their place, however, people will pay for online courses because of the following reasons:

1. **The date of the physical training not being convenient for them**
    Physical trainings usually have a fixed date when they are held. This automatically means that there are a set of people who might not be able to attend because the date is not convenient for them.

    People are juggling a number of responsibilities, and even though they really want to attend the training, they may not be able to attend it.

    If there is an online course that can take them through the training, they will gladly take it because it's usually not time-bound and they can take it at a time convenient for them.

2. **The location of the physical training not being convenient for them**

Physical trainings usually have a fixed location, which means that there are a number of people who will not be able to attend the training because it's too far from them.

There are a few exceptions who can travel any distance in the search for knowledge, but the truth remains that, a large population cannot afford to travel every time there is a training they want to attend.

If these people had access to an online course, they would gladly pay for it because they can readily gain access to the internet.

3. **The duration of the physical training not being convenient for them**

Some people find it difficult to attend physical trainings because they are have certain responsibilities that they have to attend to.

For instance, employees engaged in a 9-5 job might not be able to attend a 3- day workshop, without getting approval from their organizations.

Mothers who have to do school runs might not be able to attend a full day training, but will appreciate an online course which they can watch whenever they can carve out the time to.

These set of people would appreciate an online course that allows them to go through the training at their own convenience.

4. **They don't want to be overwhelmed**

Physical trainings can be overwhelming because the facilitator is usually trying to share so much information within a short period of time.

While this is great, people assimilate information differently. Some people are slower than others and would appreciate if the training could be delivered in bits so they can assimilate one layer of information before the next is added.

Online courses offer this flexibility because a student can watch a lesson over and over again, until they understand it.

5. **They want ongoing support**

A number of people can testify that when they attend a physical training, it's usually an exhilarating time. However, this feeling disappears after a few days. Sometimes, attendees even forget what they had learnt.

People are now craving for a training program that will offer them additional support as they implement.
They want to be able to ask questions and get feedback as they implement the lessons.

They want to be a part of a community and to form strong connections with other people who are on the same journey with them.

How are Online Courses Different From Free Content Like YouTube Videos?

Free content like YouTube videos, livestreams, and so on are used to share information, educate people about a concept, create desire for a result etc. but information alone does not always help people to get results.

Information alone does not always help people to get results.

When people watch the free content, they may still have follow-up questions or may need some form of hand-holding, personalized feedback and accountability especially when they are learning a new skill for the first time.

With an online course, you can offer this level of support, which is not readily available with free content.

How are Online Courses Different From Online Coaching?

Coaching is a more intimate relationship because a coach works with a client exclusively to help them achieve a specific result.

Due to the nature of the relationship, a coach can only work with a few people at a time and the price of this service is typically high. For example, coaches can charge from $1,000 to as high as $10,000 for a package and may only work with 4 to 6 people at a time.

On the other hand, online courses allow people to help many clients at the same time to get specific results. It's a more scalable way of working with people. The best part is, you only have to create a course once, and you can keep selling it over and over again. The price of an online course can range from $27 to $3,000 depending on the type of course you are creating.

You don't even have to be a coach to create an online course.

Online courses are really about teaching a skill you know quite well or sharing a valuable experience that you have. You just have to give yourself the permission to help other people succeed by sharing your wisdom with them.

Success Story

I wasn't sure of what to expect when I joined the Course Launched Delivered course.

I had doubts but I was certain about learning something new.

2 modules into the course, I got clarity on my course title and before the course was over, I became certain of the best way to present my own online course. Prior to the course, I wasn't tech savvy but the video lessons made techy stuff as simple as ABC and now I can say I'm 7/10 when it comes to tech stuff.

Course Launched Delivered did not only empower me to launch my own online course, but also equipped me to do a whole lot more.... like building my email list to 1200, learning how to communicate the value of my course, knowing how to network in the social space and so many other things.

I launched my online course, The Profitable Manufacturer, which helps entrepreneurs to build profitable businesses on the 15th of December 2017 and I got a total of 29 students. What gives me joy is the fact that I'm able to guide a lot of people in the manufacturing space from the comfort of my room and they in turn get all the information needed in the comfort of their spaces.

All of these achievements were made possible because Stephanie, "the quintessential online course coach", was on board holding me by the hand to ensure that I got it right. She is one of my 2017 miracles and I'm forever grateful.

Don't worry about your topic, content, presentation style, or delivery. All will be as simple as ABC after Course Launched Delivered.

Bola Adefila
The Profitable Manufacturer
www.bolaadefila.com

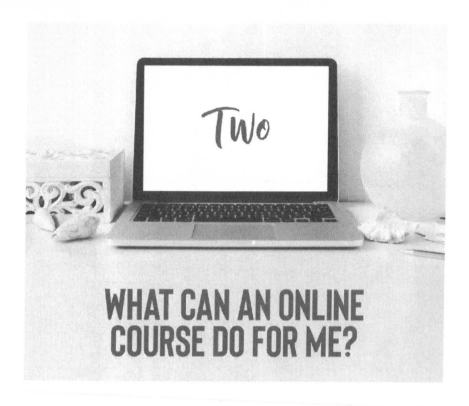

WHAT CAN AN ONLINE COURSE DO FOR ME?

When I think about that widow in the Bible who had the jar of oil and was still in debt, I get so emotional because I realise that she did not know what her jar of oil could do for her.

It's the same thing with online courses.

Many people have not yet created their online courses because they have not seen what online courses can do for them.

As you read this chapter, my prayer is that the scales will fall off your eyes.

An online course can change your life and the lives of your students, but you have to see the potential first otherwise you won't be encouraged to make a move.

If you haven't seen a clear picture of how online courses can change your life, it will always sound like a nice idea that you keep flirting with, an item that's on your to-do list, or a goal that you keep abandoning after you start.

Here are several things you can achieve when you launch your online course:

It can help you to earn an extra stream of income

An online course is a product that you can sell as a side hustle or in addition to the other services you provide.

I created my first online course while I was still fully employed in a 9 to 5 job, and the course did not disturb my job because it was completely online. I didn't have to be physically present anywhere to deliver it.

Here is the more interesting part about making money from online courses: You can resell your courses over and over and over again.

It's like building a house and receiving house rent from the tenants over and over again as the years go by.

You only have to do the work once, and money will consistently flow into your bank account anytime you launch.

To some people, this means that they can make more money so that they can send their children to a better school.

To other people, it means that they can move houses.

To some people, it means that can go on a vacation without worrying about what's left in their bank account.

To others, it means that they can give generously to their favourite charity or religious organization.

It can help you to reach more people

An online course allows you to reach people who need your help, irrespective of where they live.

When you launch a physical training program, you're automatically limited to the number of people who live in the location where you launch and its environs.

In some cases, you might be teaching a niche topic that might not have a wide audience in the city you live in. In other cases, the people who need to attend your class might not be available on the day on the event.

When you create an online course, you can attract more clients from different locations and this makes your income potential limitless. You can also attract clients who would not have been able to attend your physical training because they have another event planned for that day.

Course creators have literally made 2 to 10 times what they used to earn before, simply because they created an online course that was bought by hundreds and even thousands of people.

I've seen online courses that have been taken by over 40,000 people in over 130 countries, and the number keeps growing every year.

It can help you to move locations and still earn an income

Online courses allow you to work from anywhere because your physical location does not matter.

Many businesses die when the owners has to move, especially if the business had a physical location or its customers were tied to a particular location.

I had a client whose husband was moving to a different country and they decided that she would also move. This meant that she had to pack up her business or leave it in the care of a manager who may or may not run the business properly.

It also meant that she had to start again in this new city she was relocating to. She survived this transition by creating an online course.

If you have an online course, you can literally continue like nothing ever happened.

You don't even need to be in the same time zone with the people taking your course.

It can help you to have some flexibility in your life

Online courses allow you to be flexible with your schedule.

You can decide that you want to be a stay-at-home mum, take care of your kids, and still make money by selling online courses.

You can decide that you only want to work a certain number of hours per day or at certain times in the day.

You can decide that you want to travel to different countries all year round.

You can decide to take the day off to spend with a friend who just dropped by or with your kids.

You can do all these and it won't affect you if you have an online course that earns you money.

There are even stories of people dealing with illnesses like depression and cancer, or people who get into an accident and have to spend time recuperating in the hospital, but can comfortably pay their bills because they have an online course that is set up to bring them income.

Whatever your reason is, online courses can help you create flexibility and freedom to live your life the way you want to.

You only have one life and you are living it right now. If you are complaining everyday about what's happening in your life, remember that you have the ability to change your life, unlike trees that can't help themselves.

You can design a life that makes you happy and use online courses as a source of income.

You can design a life that makes you happy and use online courses as a source of income.

It can help you to become recognized as an expert on your topic

When you create an online course, it shows that you are an authority on your topic. This can lead to you being invited to speak at conferences, summits, etc.

You can use it as a follow up product

This is particularly relevant to established speakers, authors and experts, who speak at various events. Many times, the 30 to 60 minutes you have been given to speak is usually not enough to help people to actually get the results they are looking for.

You can use an online course as an opportunity to present an upsell to people who want to learn more about your topic after your presentation.

You can use it to take advantage of the huge gap in the market

Not every topic is being taught in schools, and so there is already a huge gap in the market, and a group of people already looking for trainings in topics they can't find anywhere else.

If you launch a topic in a field where there is a huge gap, you will find a waiting list of people who are ready to pay for your course even before you finish working on it.

It can help you to save time

If you've tried to train people before, you might find yourself saying the same thing to people over and over again.

If you are really good at what you do, you are going to get more requests to train as your popularity grows. In the beginning, it might be okay to explain things to people one after the other, but when the number of requests grows, you might find that you are spending so much time explaining the same thing to different people all the time.

You can save yourself the time and effort it takes to repeat yourself over and over again by creating an online course that answers all their questions and helps them to achieve the results they really want.

It can help you prevent burn out.

A common challenge that passionate people who want to impact lives face is that they just keep going and they don't realise when other areas of their lives such as their health or family life start to deteriorate or suffer.

Some others get overwhelmed by the number of people that come to them for help.

With online courses, you can balance things out.

You can have a hugely successful business and still have work-life balance.

It can give you a great sense of fulfilment

Money is great but the fulfilment you get from actually impacting the lives of other people is just priceless and the impact is usually beyond the tangible results that we can all see and measure.

I will give you an example:

Let's say you create an online course to help married women with kids to lose weight.

You obviously will make money when your ideal client pays for her course, but there's more:

First, you've made her to look more attractive to her husband and you might just be saving her marriage. She now looks attractive once again and romance can be rekindled in her relationship with her husband.

Second, you've made her fit enough to play with her children. There are some overweight women who can't run around with their children; the excess weight gets them easily fatigued. They lose out on priceless moments because they can't run around and play with their kids. For women like these, the value of losing weight, keeping fit and being healthy enough for their children, is priceless. It's just priceless.

Third, you've boosted her self esteem and she now feels confident. This confidence will affect other areas of her life and she might start doing better at work or in her business. She might start taking on leadership positions because she feels confident.

All these are happening simply because she took an online course to lose weight.

The feeling you will get when she describes how much you helped to change her life is priceless.

Industry Trends that Show Why You Need to Create an Online Course Now

1. It's already a billion dollar industry

According to Forbes, the online education industry was valued to be a $107 billion industry in 2015. This global e-learning market is also expected to reach $225 billion in 2017 according to the World Economic Forum and it's going to keep growing.

This shows that people are already paying to consume trainings on the go. There is already a huge demand for online courses.

This industry is however still in the infancy stage, and it will keep growing.

This is the time to take advantage of this opportunity.

2. Easy access to the internet

Smartphones and data are getting cheaper. This is enabling the rate of internet penetration, and with smartphones, a lot more people can now access the internet to find information to help them with personal development.

3. It is already a proven business model

If you are just learning about online courses for the first time, you might be a bit sceptical about the profitability of this venture.

According to Teachable, an online education platform that hosts online courses, on the average, an instructor makes $5,426 and that's for a beginner.

More experienced instructors earn 7 figures in dollars and this makes up a significant part of their revenue.

This suggests that people are already making money from creating their own online courses.

4. Developments in the tech space

A lot of things that used to be very difficult to do are now very easy, because of the advancements in technology products.

For instance, it used to be very expensive to host an online course, but today there are platforms that can host your entire online course for you.

There are also a lot of easy-to-use tools you can now use to launch your course.

5. Deep thirst for knowledge

There is a huge demand for knowledge and people are always looking for one form of information or the other.

The opportunity here is that, there will always be a set of people in any given market who wants answers to their questions and are willing to pay someone who has done all the research, made all the mistakes, experimented and gotten results, to show them how to get results in an organised step-by-step manner, even though there's so much information on the internet. They want a shortcut.

There will always be a set of people in any given market who wants answers to their questions and are willing to pay someone who has done all the research, made all the mistakes, experimented, gotten results, to just show them how to get results in an organised step by step manner, even though there's so much information on the internet. They want a shortcut.

Success Story

"I could only work with two people at a time"

My name is Ijeoma Ndukwe, popularly known as Nwanyi Akamu, and I sell pap. I run a food processing and packaging company called Bubez Foods, but I have a deep passion for empowering female entrepreneurs. I help them to get clarity over their brands and what they need to do to build sustainable businesses.

People started coming to me from afar to help with their brand strategy, but I could only work with two people at a time due to my tight schedule. I found myself turning back the people I was passionate about. I knew that there had to be a way to help more people.

I reached out to Stephanie Obi, the teacher of online courses. I paid for her programme, learnt her Course Launched Delivered method and delivered my own online course.

In two months, I earned $13,000 from my first online course. I now have over 50 students enrolled in my online course from all over the world.

Ijeoma Ndukwe
Pap Seller and Brand Strategist
www.bubezcentre.org

Exercise

Why do you want to create your own online course?

_____

_____

_____

_____

What will change in your life after you create your online course?

_____

_____

_____

WHAT CAN I TEACH?

I was once asked this question, "What can I teach? and I said, "You can teach a topic that you are very passionate about".

The person responded, "I'm very passionate about eating, can I teach that?"

We all laughed out loud about it but what if I told you that you can actually teach an online course on eating?

There are several - not one - several online courses that teach people how to eat.
I'm not even kidding.

If you google "eating online course", you will see a lot of online courses that have been created on the topic and they even have testimonials.
The truth is, there is actually so much that you can teach because there is so much you already know.

In life, we have a lot of teachable moments. These are moments in our past where we learnt something very valuable. The only problem is that we tend to take these experiences for granted.

In some other cases, we have things that come to us easily, and we assume that other people know these things. We often don't realise that there are so many people struggling to learn these same things that we take for granted.

We all have different skill sets and different experiences, that we can teach others as there are always people who are trying to learn these same things we know.

The topic you can teach and get paid for might surprise you.

You Can Teach a Practical Skill You Have Acquired

I once launched a wildly successful online course where I was teaching entrepreneurs how to design graphics with Canva. This is a skill I sat down to learn after getting frustrated by graphic designers. I discovered that other people were also struggling with the same issue.

Lucy Adi came into the Course Launched Delivered online course without a clear idea of what she wanted to teach. When we ran the brainstorming exercise, she realised that she could teach people how to build websites.

She had taught herself to build have websites when she decided to build one for her own business. Upon further investigation, she found out that there were so many business owners who did not have a website because they claimed that web designers were too expensive or that they wanted their websites to be designed in certain ways which they could not really articulate to the web designers. They wanted to be able to design their own websites but did not know how to.

Lucy successfully launched her online course, teaching business owners how to create their own websites and she is even being invited now to speak at events as an expert.

You Can Teach a Gift You Have

When Adeola Babatunde wanted to launch her first online course, she started off with a particular idea. As we worked on validating this idea in the Course Launched Delivered online course, we discovered that there were not a lot of people who wanted to pay to learn this topic. In fact, nobody had ever paid her to teach this topic. We started to explore her other gifts, and we discovered that she had a gift for delivering presentations.

She always used to get a lot of compliments and standing ovations anytime she made presentations, but it had never occurred to her that she could actually teach this topic as a course. She even struggled with the idea of launching an online course on something that came to her so easily.

After some soul searching, she went ahead to launch her course, "Confident Presentation Formula", and so many opportunities have opened up for her because people now recognise her as an expert in this topic. Some of these opportunities are:

• She got an opportunity to speak at a bank

- She has been training at different organizations
- She has started working one-on-one with high profile individuals

As if this was not enough, one of her students who had taken her online course told her that she got a promotion after making a presentation.

Glory Edozien, another lady I worked with to launch her online course, was always getting compliments on her networking skills, and she didn't see it as a big deal because it came to her naturally. Networking had helped her to get in front of very influential contacts who recommended her as a local policy expert to contribute to Nigeria's foremost climate change policy document.

In addition to this, she had organised more than 10 women empowerment events with over 500 women in attendance. All these events had notable and influential speakers, all of whom she met through networking.

She discovered that this gift which came to her so naturally did not come as naturally to other women. Each time she attended events, she noticed that women only spoke to their friends, didn't know how to start conversations and felt awkward about following up with new contacts, and so she decided to create an online course to teach this skill.

You Can Teach a Lesson You Gained From an Experience

Bola Adefila had been involved in her family's tissue paper manufacturing business, Banrut Rolls, since its inception. She realised that she had built up a wealth of experience when it came to manufacturing and could help other manufacturers to become profitable.

She launched her online course, "The Profitable Manufacturer" and still works in her family's manufacturing business.

Remi Owadokun once weighed 110kg and had so many health complications. She had high blood pressure, high cholesterol levels, pre-diabetes, hormonal imbalance and always had migraines. Not to mention that she looked 10 years older than her real age.

She decided to change her lifestyle and lost 40kg naturally without going to the gym or working with a personal trainer. In addition to that, all the health complications disappeared and she went from taking pills everyday to not taking any more pills.

Today, after coaching over 200 people one-on-one, she has created an online school, and put up an online course in order to scale her business and to help other people who are trying to lose weight and are going through similar struggles such as denial, food addiction, inconsistency, etc.

She was forced to start sharing her knowledge when she hit rock bottom. She only had N10 left in her pockets. Her rent was due and she was running out of food.

This forced her to look within to find what she could monetize.

You don't have to get to rock bottom before you start making money from your life experiences. You can start today.

It's your turn.

Look through the examples below and complete the brainstorming exercise to find possible course ideas that you can teach. The list is endless.

Exercise

Get a pen and notebook and list out every idea that comes into your mind in answering the questions below.

As you answer them, you might have some ideas that sound stupid.
Don't edit your answers...just write the first thing that pops into your head.

We will spend time evaluating the answers later, but for now, just get the ideas out of your head.

You can have multiple answers for one question; allow the answers to flow.

1. **What questions do people always ask you?**

   Try to recall the compliments you always receive. You may not realise it, but you keep doing something that other people admire and they may want to learn how you are doing it.

   Examples:
   How did you lose weight?
   You are very good at networking, how do you do it?

   _____

   ....

2. **What painful experience have you overcome?**

   For any emotionally painful experience you successfully overcame, you most likely learnt a lot from it.

   There are other people who are going through that same painful experience and are looking for help.

   They will even listen to you because you deeply understand what they are going through, and you won't judge them. Instead, you will give them practical tips on what they can do to get the results that they want. You will even know the exact examples, illustrations, relevant lessons, exercises and resource guides to come up with when you are creating your content.

Exercise

Examples:
Failing certification exams and finally passing them after the third attempt.
Finally getting a job after not able to succeed in job interviews for three years.

_____

_____

3. **What exciting goal have you achieved?**

For every goal you have achieved, there are tons of people who want to achieve that goal but are struggling.
They are even beginning to look like failures because they have not achieved that goal.

Don't take your achievements for granted, no matter how small they may seem.

Examples:
I wrote a book in 10 days
I ran a marathon

_____

_____

4. **What tools do you know how to use very well?**

The more sophisticated a tool is, the more difficult it is to learn how to use it.

If you have spent a lot of time mastering how to use a tool, I can bet that there are a lot of people out there who don't want to spend the length of time you have invested learning how to use that tool...they want a shortcut instead.

Examples:
Learning to use a video camera
Learning to use a sewing machine

_____

_____

5. **What do you spend so much time researching on?**

Chances are, if you spend time learning about something, you know a lot more than the average person about that topic. Not everybody will have the time to read all the books you've read. They might not even know how to apply all the information they've come across online.

If you have researched a topic, applied it, and gotten results, people will be willing to pay you to teach them how to get the same results.

Examples:
Researching how to use tech tools
Learning about nutrition and how to cook healthy meals

_____

_____

6. **What software or web application do you know how to use very well?**

Once again, you have probably invested a lot of time learning how to use certain software or web applications or web application and there are many people who don't want to spend all that time. You can also create a course to teach them so that they will save time.

Examples:
Teaching how to use Microsoft Excel
Teaching how to use Photoshop _____

_____

7. **What skill have you learnt?**

If there's a skill you have gained mastery of, you can also teach other people how to learn this skill.

Examples:
Playing the piano

_____

_____

41

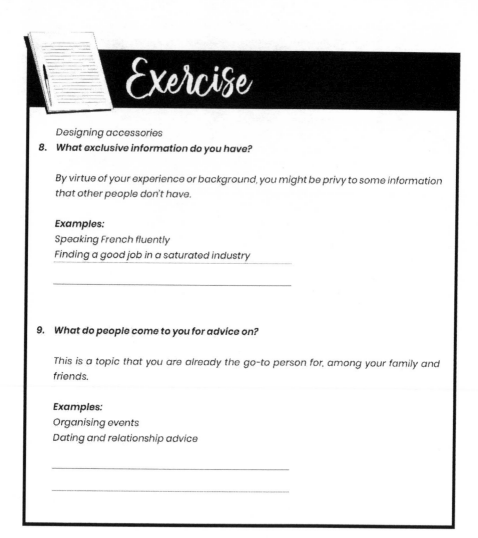

Designing accessories

8. What exclusive information do you have?

By virtue of your experience or background, you might be privy to some information that other people don't have.

Examples:
Speaking French fluently
Finding a good job in a saturated industry

9. What do people come to you for advice on?

This is a topic that you are already the go-to person for, among your family and friends.

Examples:
Organising events
Dating and relationship advice

The list is endless.

You will discover that you have more than enough topics that you can create an online course on. Your next problem will be "which topic do I pick?"

We will address this question in a different chapter.
Sit tight.

WHY PEOPLE PAY FOR ONLINE COURSES

This is a million dollar question, because I have seen so many people hold themselves back from launching their online courses because they can't see why anyone will pay for their online course when they can get the information for free online.

Before I resolve this issue, I just want to take the time to explain to you that people are already paying for online courses.

This is not a business model I'm proposing that might work; it is an already established business model that works.

Despite all the information that is already available for free online, people still pay for online courses and here are several reasons why:

1. **They want results**
    People are looking for results, not information.

    It's one thing to have information, and it's a completely different ball game to be able to turn that information into results.

If they wanted information, they would have googled or asked their friends. But people want results and they need somebody who has gotten the same results they are looking for, and can show them how to get them.

If you can package your online course to help people get the specific result they are looking for, they will pay for it and will spread the good news about your course.

2.   **They want to save time**
Some people are tired of trying to figure things out by themselves and wasting time learning by trial and error.

I personally believe that anybody can figure out anything by themselves. The question is "when will they figure out?" Many businesses have failed because the owners did not figure out the solutions to their problems on time, and they could not afford the expensive mistakes they were making.

I personally believe that anybody can figure
out anything by themselves.
The question is when will they figure it out?

In addition to this, there are also some people who don't want to learn a new skill from scratch. According to research, for someone to master a skill, they must spend 10,000 hours developing themselves in that topic.

Not everybody wants to spend 10,000 hours gaining knowledge on a topic, so they would prefer to pay someone else who has already spent 10,000 hours and can tell them exactly what they need to know to get the results that they seek.

In the same vein, not everybody wants to spend so much time on search engines, looking through the 50 million entries that come up when they search for a topic.

3.   **They want to save money**

Some people have already lost money because they made mistakes. They don't want to make any more costly mistakes.

Sometimes, they can't afford a professional who charges premium charges, so they would prefer to take an online course which is a more affordable option.

For example, to hire a web designer can cost anywhere from $500 to $2,000. An entrepreneur can decide to take a $299 course that will teach him how to design his website and still get some support instead of hiring a professional to design it for him.

4.   They want to build relationships
Some people will pay for your course because they want to build a relationship with you.

They want you to share their success stories, to get your feedback on certain topics and to be able to ask you for favours later, etc.

Some others want to take your course because they are looking for new networking opportunities. They probably want to meet new people, change their circles or surround themselves with the types of people who can help them to achieve their goals.

Some people feel very lonely on the path they are on, especially if they don't have people around them physically who understand the journey they are on or can even answer the questions that they have.

If you build a strong community as one of the features of your course, people will be attracted to it because they want to be a part of that community.

People have met business partners in an online course community and gone ahead to launch products and events together.

Some have found accountability partners who they can share their struggles with, who will support them and not judge them.

5.   They want your perspective
Some people like the way you do things and want to learn from you, even though there are other people who are teaching the same topic you teach.

Some people like what is different about you. They probably like the way you speak, the way you think or the way you break things down, among other things.

Sometimes it could even be the fact that you have something in common. For example, if you are married and your ideal clients are married, they might resonate with you more because they feel that you might be able to empathise with them more.

A good number of my clients have said to me, "I've paid for a course on how to create online courses before, but I just discovered that I can relate with you better; that's why I paid for your course".

6. **They want to learn from credible people**
When you create an online course, you put your face behind the course and you tell the world, "I have achieved this and I can show you how to achieve this if you take my online course"

People are looking for people who are credible and can stand behind their results.

There are a lot of quacks online who sell information products because they want to make a quick buck. Some people will even copy and paste things they copied online, put it together and call it an online course.

This happens because the real people who have results have not launched their online courses and people who are desperate for results fall for scams.

If you have results to show and you launch your online course, there are already people waiting for you because they trust you.

7. **They want guidance**
Some people want you to SHOW them, not TELL them what to do. They know what to do but for some reason, they still are not getting results. They don't know what they don't know. They feel stuck and are ready for some hand-holding.

They need some level of guidance, motivation, accountability and support so that they will not be stranded when they get stuck again.

8. They want a step-by-step solution

Some people want a well arranged step-by-step solution delivered sequentially. They want to know the first step they should take, and then the second and so on.

They have tried googling the topic online and listening to so many free trainings, but they just ended up getting overwhelmed with all the information.

They just want someone to tell them what to do, when and how.

9. They can't find a solution anywhere else

Believe it or not, not all information is available for free online.

The fact that someone shares a lot of free tips online does not mean that they are sharing all that they know about that topic.

There are still trade secrets out there and there are many topics your ideal clients might be looking to learn about that have not been addressed.

In some cases, someone else may have created an online course on the topic they're interested in but didn't really go into the details.

For instance, if someone has launched a course on "Online Marketing" and did not go into details on "Facebook Ads", your ideal client might be looking for a well detailed course on Facebook Ads, and will come to you if you create one.

Success Story

*I was 7 months pregnant, but determined to launch my course...
I'm super glad I didn't wait till conditions were better to do it! I'm proud of myself and convinced that if it worked for me, it can work for anyone.*

I was 7 months pregnant, but determined to launch my course.
Steph's Course Launched Delivered method was easy to follow and her voice of encouragement was always ringing in my ears.

To be honest, I chose the simplest of every option she gave for the launch stages because of my tired state.

The thing is, it still worked!

I rounded up my first launch and got my first set of students. I also got more clients for my consulting packages and requests to organize content training for staff during my launch.

I'm sitting in my living room in Port Harcourt smiling as students review my course and send in testimonials. I have students from Lagos, Enugu, Atlanta, and many more places. People have even started joining the waiting list for the next time I relaunch the course.

My work and sacrifice were worth it!

I'm super glad I didn't wait till conditions were better to do it! I'm proud of myself and convinced that if it worked for me, it can work for anyone.

It was my passion to teach what I knew that led me to Course Launched Delivered, but today it is a major stream of income in my business and I'm impacting people in places beyond my physical reach.

The Course Launched Delivered online course paid for itself, all other costs and then some.

Thank you Steph!
Tolu Michaels
www.tolumichaels.com

Multiply Your Sales with Words

A step-by-step guide for writing content that turns Social Media Scrollers and Likers into paying customers

is now live

Visit
TOLUMICHAELS.COM/COURSES
to signup

Five

WHO CAN CREATE AN ONLINE COURSE?

I remember reading a message from a lady.

I'm not a coach, she said. I don't have any certifications.

I just know that I'm good at what I do, and people are always coming to me for help.

Can I also create an online course?
She was puzzled because she didn't feel like she had the permission to teach others.
The sad part is, she is not alone.

For some reason, we have come to believe that wisdom is reserved for a certain few and that only a few people can teach. We believe that the rest of us don't know anything at all. We are all supposed to keep quiet, never teach anybody, stand by and watch the "privileged few" who are allowed to teach.

Of course, this is not true.

We are all capable of teaching.

In the past, we might not have gotten opportunities to teach on a large scale because there were gatekeepers who restricted the people who had access to platforms.

Things have however changed because we now have the internet and can create our own platforms.

This is one reason online education is exploding.

The barriers have been broken down and anybody who believes that they have something to share with the world can freely share.

Their audience is not even restricted to the city they live in; people all over the world can find them online and learn from them.

Can you see what I'm trying to explain to you?

You too can create an online course.

I know that you might feel uncomfortable with the idea of calling yourself an expert, but here's how to look at it.

An expert is someone who is very knowledgeable about a particular topic. It could be cooking, cleaning, dressing fashionably, etc. It does not have to be a hard core topic or you can only learn in a formal institution.

If there's something you do all the time, you are probably very knowledgeable about that topic and can easily teach it.

Here are some examples of people who can easily create online courses based on what they do everyday:

1. **Service-Based Entrepreneurs**
    There are people who cannot afford your highly priced package, but still want to learn from you. For example, if you are a premium-priced wedding planner, there are probably many people who cannot afford your service but they might be willing to learn how to plan their weddings by themselves using your methodology.

    You can even get to a point where you want to teach aspiring entrepreneurs how to succeed in your industry. For example, if you have built a successful fashion business, aspiring fashion designers would be reaching out to you for mentorship, and they will be more keen on learning from you because you have achieved the type of success they are dreaming about.

This is exactly what happened to one of my clients, Ayotomi Rotimi. She is a veteran in the fashion industry in Nigeria and has built a thriving ready-to-wear brand for women, Xclamations!

She found that she was always giving advice to people in the industry because a lot of her colleagues consider her as a go-to person as she has been at it for so long.

She came on the Course Launched Delivered program because she wanted to help more fashion designers to build profitable businesses. Developing an online course was a way to scale up her impact and still be rewarded for her wealth of expertise.

2. Coaches

There's a limit to how many people coaches can work with one-on-one, and that automatically places a limit on their income potential. For example, if your one-on-one coaching package is $1,000 and you can only work with 10 people per month, this limits your income.

However, if you convert some of the lessons you take people through and package them as an online course, you unlock endless opportunities.

You no longer have to sell your time or feel like you are locked to your laptop or office.

3. Consultants

Consultants are very knowledgeable in their area of expertise, and they spend a lot of time helping their clients get results. They offer a premium service and can only work with a limited number of clients at a time.

If you are a consultant, there probably is a different demographic that needs your expertise and you can still earn an income from serving that market. For instance, you may consult for banks but you could open up to a new demographic such as entrepreneurs. These entrepreneurs may not be able to afford your consultancy fee but could afford your online course.

A great example is Steve Harris. He is a successful management consultant who has led consulting interventions in many top companies in Nigeria. He however had a strong desire to help upcoming entrepreneurs who knew that they had a gift but were struggling to turn their gift into a successful business. He launched his online course, "Mastering the Business of your Talent", and that course has helped over 300 people to launch their businesses.

4.   **Product-Based Entrepreneurs**
If you have developed your own line of products, you might be able to teach people a skill you've developed in the course of building your business.

For instance, if you have a line of baby food products, you can teach mothers how to prepare meals for their babies. As a bonus, you can also use your products as you are teaching how to prepare the meals.

One of my clients, Dr Chinny Obinwanne sells low calorie cookies, granola and smoothie mixes to help mothers increase their breast milk supply through her business, The Milk Booster, but discovered that some mothers struggled with producing enough milk to exclusively breastfeed their newborn babies. She had been teaching a lot of mothers freely but realised that she was limited because of time. So, she decided to create an online course to reach more mothers.

5.   **Authors**
If you have written a book, you already have an audience who wants to consume more of your content. You can create an online course that deep-dives into the topics you raised in your book and can offer your clients additional support.

6.   **Bloggers, Vloggers, Podcasters and Facebook Group Owners**
If you have built an audience of people who listen to you, you are already a trusted adviser and they will pay for your online course if you create one.

John Obidi is the founder of Smart B-Camp, which has a growing Facebook group community of over 70,000 entrepreneurs. He has a knack for all things online marketing, online businesses, web and app development, live streaming, etc.

He would spend so many hours trying to figure things out, and get so much fulfilment from sharing what he had learnt with the members of his community for free.

In 2014, he decided to monetise one of the things he would usually teach for free. He created his first online course, "How to Make Money Creating Apps", and was amazed at the results. He still serves his community with free resources they can use to grow their businesses but has gone ahead to create more online courses.

7. Trainers

If you already organize live events where you train on your topic, there are tons of people interested in what you teach who cannot travel to your city. If you make your training programme available online, they will pay for it

One of my clients, Phinnah Chichi Ikeji, felt limited because most of her trainings were offline and location-based. She organises workshops aimed at motivating teenagers and helping them to acquire life skills. She, however, found that parents found it difficult to bring their teenagers to her events. When she created her online courses, the parents no longer had to struggle with bringing their teens to all her events; they could just watch the videos at home, at a time that was convenient for them.

8. Hobbyists

If you have spent so much time learning a particular hobby, you have fellow hobbyists who would be interested in learning from you because they are passionate about it too and want guidance.

9. 9–5ers

This is the ultimate side hustle because you don't even have to be physically present to deliver the product.

There are many things that 9-5ers can teach. It can be a skill you learnt on the job, a hobby you have developed on the side or a topic you like to research on.

Tomie Balogun had a consulting job in a firm, but realised that after working for 4 years, she did not have any savings. She decided to form an investment club with 4 of her friends. When they started, they thought that all they had to do was to put their money together and to start investing in profitable investment opportunities but they were so wrong. They had to do a lot of studying and seek advice from industry experts.

With time, they built up a stock portfolio, invested in fixed income securities, foreign exchange and multiple small businesses in three industries. This experience taught her a lot about investing and then people started reaching out to her for advice on how to invest in the Nigerian market.

She decided to create an online course and today, she makes over 3 times her monthly salary from her online courses. She has also transited from her 9-5 and she is now building a Fintech company to enable simple investing for every Nigerian.

10. **Mentors**

Mentorship is a relationship where a more experienced person in a field or industry helps to guide a less experienced person.

Mentors usually have to invest a lot of time with their mentees and this automatically means that there's a limit to how many people they can effectively mentor.

If a lot of people keep coming to you for mentorship, you can create an online course on the specific areas that they keep coming to you for advice on.

Tara Fela-Durotoye is a celebrated beauty entrepreneur who pioneered the bridal make-up profession in Nigeria. Her company, House of Tara International grew from a passion to a business that now has 23 branches, over 10,000 beauty representatives and over 100 employees. They have a presence in most major cities across the country, distribution channels in Ghana, Kenya, Rwanda and a plan to expand to other cities in Africa, Europe and North America. One of the questions aspiring mentees kept asking her was how they could structure their businesses.

My platform, _www.trayny.com_ which creates and hosts online courses from Africa's most trusted leaders, approached her to help create an online course for her so that she could effectively reach the people who kept coming to her for help. The first time we launched the course, we got close to 150 students from over 9 countries.

ONLINE COURSE

www.trayny.com/structure

11. **Stay-at-Home Mums**

If you are a mother who has made the decision to stay at home for some years to take care of your kids, you can also launch an online course.

12. **Speakers**

When you go on speaking engagements, there is only so much you can share within the 30 or 60 minutes allotted to you.

If you create an online course, you can continue serving your audience and help them to achieve their goals. You can also earn an additional stream of income.

As you read through the different types of people who can create online courses, I'm sure you may have noticed one common thread: they all have knowledge that other people are interested in learning. If you know something that other people are trying to learn, please create your online course.

HOW TO MAKE MONEY FROM ONLINE COURSES

I was speaking to a guy, and he asked, "So, what do you do?"

"I create and sell online courses" , I replied.

"Really? Do you make money? Why don't you go and do another business?"

I just began laughing. I had no words.

Let me tell you, online courses are one of the most versatile products I've seen because you can make money from them in so many different ways and at many different times.

The best way to describe this is to liken it to building a house.

When you build a house and you let it out, you can keep receiving rental income from it year after year. You don't have to do any other thing to keep receiving that income.

You might decide to renovate the house at some point, but after you do, you can still keep receiving rental income from it for the rest of your life. You can even will it to your children.

This is almost too good to be true because you do not have to work yourself into the ground.

You only have to do all the work upfront and once that is done, you can keep making money from it in so many different ways.

1. **You can sell your online course all year round.**
   Once you have your online course set up, it can become a stream of passive income all year round as people can discover your online course at different times during the year and can decide to pay for it whenever they like.

   You can also easily set up a marketing funnel that directs people to your online course. You can direct people to it any time you go out on speaking engagements or anytime someone approaches you for help.

   You can also run special promotions around your course at different times to drive sales. For instance you can have an "it's my birthday" sale, a Christmas bundle or a Valentine's day offer.

   A lot of people use their online courses to raise quick cash when they have an emergency. You can easily do this by offering a special promotion on one of your online courses or bundling two or more online courses together and selling it at a discount for a limited time. You can also give extra bonuses if you are not comfortable with discounts. Many of the members of your community will jump on it because everybody loves a good deal.

2. **You can relaunch your course over and over again.**
   Another way to make money through online courses is to open your course for enrolment for a limited number of days, and then open it up again at another time.

   For instance, you can launch your online course in January, and get some customers. Then, you can relaunch it in April, in September and in December.

   You can still relaunch it multiple times the following year.

The reason this works is that the members of your community are in different places. Some people may not have been ready for your course the first time you launched it, but they might be ready to pay for it the second or third time you launch it.

Some people may not have heard about you the first time you launched the course, but as you grow your community, they may find out about you and pay for your online course the next time you launch it.

This is the beauty of online courses.

You can keep earning more money as your influence grows.

Here's an illustration.

Scenario 1:

You launch a mini course priced at $97

The first time you launch it, you can get 10 customers:
$97* 10 customers = $970

The second time you launch it, you can get 20 customers:
$97 * 20 customers = $1,940

The third time you launch it, you can get 35 customers:
$97 * 35 customers = $3,395

The fourth time you launch it, you can get 40 customers:
$97 * 40 customers = $3,880

Total: $10,185

Scenario 2:

You launch a course priced at $497

The first time you launch it, you can get 10 customers:
$497* 10 customers = $4,970

The second time you launch it, you can get 20 customers:
$497 * 20 customers = $9,940

Total: $14,910

The earlier you launch your course, the more money you can potentially make because the first set of people who take your course will share testimonials of the results they got while on your course.

This will, in turn, grow your influence and encourage more people to take your course the next time you launch. You can even increase the price of your course as you relaunch it.

This is why it's so important to launch your course now.

Don't compare yourself with another influencer who launched a course and got over 500 students. Everybody starts from zero. Start today and start building up.

3. **You can make money from online courses by setting up a joint venture partnership.**
    A joint venture partnership is a temporary partnership where two or more individuals (or companies) come together to achieve a particular goal.

    In this case, the goal will be to sell your online course to more people.

    There are different types of joint venture partnerships you can get into:

    You can have an online course + online course partnership

    This is when you create your online course and then go into partnership with someone else who also has an online course, to create a special bundle that will only be available for a limited time.

    You can then offer the bundle at a great discount or you can ask people to buy the two courses for the price of one.

At the end of the promotion, you split the income with your partner at the agreed rate.

You can even take your online course on a virtual tour, partnering with other people who have an audience, and giving their community members special offers.

For every partnership to work, there has to be a win-win element for both parties involved.
In this case, both parties are winning because they are both making money from their courses.

If you offer a valuable training for free to your partner's community as you market the special bundle, it can also help your partners to build goodwill among their community members. You will also be winning because you would have gotten exposure to a brand new audience.

You can have an online course + software partnership
This is when you reach out to a software company that is related to the topic of your online course and you create a special bundle for their audience.

Let's say your course is focused on helping entrepreneurs get sales through social media. You can approach a software company whose platform helps entrepreneurs to schedule posts on social media and get into a partnership with them.

One idea is to tell them that you want to offer their community members a free training on how to use their social media tool to get more sales.

If they say yes, you will get so much exposure to a new audience who can potentially pay for your online course.

It will be a win for them because they will be providing their audience with high quality content that would help them to achieve their goals.
You can also ask the company if they will be willing to bundle a one-year subscription to their software with your online course and sell it at a discount.

This will equally be a win-win for both parties.

It's a win for you because you will be selling your online course to more people.

It will be a win for them because they will be getting more people to pay for a one-year subscription.

You can have an online course + product partnership
You can also partner with a company that sells physical products that are connected to the topic of your online course.

For instance, if your online course is about teaching busy women how to lose weight, you can partner with the producers of a certain healthy food product you recommend that they use or certain appliances they can use to prepare healthy meals.

You can have an online course + service partnership

You can also partner with an individual or a company that offers services.

For instance, if your online course is focused on helping people to write their own books, you can partner with a book cover designer or a book editor.

One of the ways you can partner with them is to ask them to give your students a special discount.

In exchange for this, you will grant them exposure to your audience. This will also be a win for you because this additional service will increase the value of your online course and more people will be encouraged to pay for it.

As you think of people to partner with, allow your mind to think outside the box and come up with names of individuals and companies who are targeting the same ideal client as you are.

You also have to think about how you can give value to the potential partners you have identified. If you approach them and they can't see how they will gain from your proposition, they might not be keen on partnering with you.

You might even have to pitch to a lot of people before you hear a yes, but keep going because the right partnerships can help you sell your online courses to a lot of people, and you won't have to start creating a new online course from scratch.

You can use an online course that you have already created.

4.   You can bring in affiliates to market your course.
An affiliate is an individual who markets your online course for you and gets a commission for every person who pays through their unique link or code.

It's a win-win for both parties as affiliates can help you to get more sales while they can get 25% - 50% commission for every sale they bring in.

When working with affiliates, look out for affiliates who have an audience who actually need your online course and can come up with a marketing plan to promote the course.

You can also provide them with some marketing resources like sample copies, tweets, talking points, and so on to help them promote your online course.

5.   You can sell your course in a market place.
Another very popular way of making money through online courses is by hosting them on online course marketplaces like Udemy or Skillshare.

A lot of new course creators host their courses on marketplaces because you can get customers from the organic traffic visiting those websites.

It's usually free to sell your courses on these platforms but they take a share of the revenue you make and they can pose several restrictions on how you can price your course, how you can communicate with your students, etc.

6.   You can sell your course to a corporate organization.

According to the 2017 Training Industry Report, over $90 billion was spent on trainings and 56% of those trainings were delivered by external facilitators just like you. You can sell multiple slots in your online course to just one corporate client and you can even create a customised online course for a corporate client.

Companies are now considering online training courses because they are a lot more convenient for their employees and also cost effective. They don't have to spend money on travel, accommodation, etc.

One thing to always remember is that you always need to link the topic of your online course to a result they are interested in.

For instance, if you have an online course focused on helping people to dress better, you can show the organisation how the way their customer-facing employees dress will affect their ability to influence customers' disposition towards the organisation, which in turn will affect their profitability.

If your course is on helping people boost their self-esteems, you can show how a lack of this can stop their employees from taking initiative, championing ideas or using their strengths to get results which would have positively impacted the company's bottom line.

For the rest of this book, we will be focusing on how to sell online courses to individuals but I just added this section to let you know that selling to corporates is also a possibility.

Exercise

How do you want to make money from your online course?

PART 2

Crush Your Mindset Blocks

The idea of creating online courses sounds exciting, but this excitement is usually dampened by limiting beliefs born of fear and self doubt.

Beliefs are very powerful. They can either make us or break us, because they are the thoughts that we believe are true.

If you look at a man's actions, you can determine what he believes because his thoughts determine the actions he takes.

If you believe that you can launch an online course which thousands of people from all over the world will take, you will waste no time in launching that online course.

If you believe that you nobody will pay for your online course, you will not launch that online course; instead you will come up with perfectly valid excuses as to why you should not go ahead and launch your online course.

The set of beliefs you have that can stop you from going ahead to launch your online course are what I describe as mindset blocks.

You might not even be aware of them, but they are there, playing around in your head, repeating their threats in your mind, screaming out loudly as you read this book.

"You cannot do it."

"People like you don't launch online courses..."

"You will just make a fool of yourself."

In this section of the book, I will expose and debunk some of the mindset blocks you might be having, so that you can confidently launch your online course.

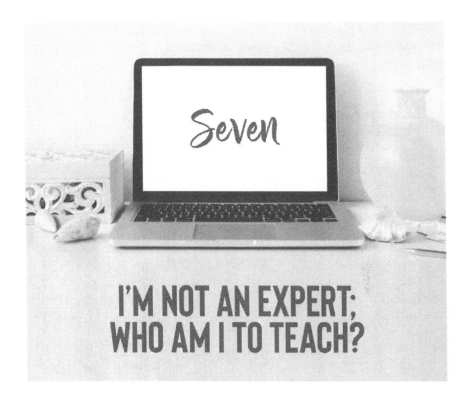

I'M NOT AN EXPERT; WHO AM I TO TEACH?

The painful part about this limiting belief is that this is a fear that most talented people have. They are always looking for how to improve themselves that they don't pause to say, "What I know is enough to teach someone".

The truth of the matter is, there will never be a point where you know it all, or a point when you don't need to learn anything new.

On the contrary, there will always be room for improvement. There will always be someone who is ahead of you. There will always be a higher level to strive for. However, as you strive to keep improving, you can help the people who are not where you are, to get there.

It's like having a ladder with ten steps.

While someone is on Step One, some other person is on Step Two, and another person is on Step Five.

The person on Step One, is looking up to the person in Step Two and saying, "Please can you help me get to Step Two?"

While the person in Step Two is looking up to the person in Step Five and saying, "Please can you help me get to Step Five?"

Teaching does not mean that you know everything; it only means that you know enough to help another person.

There will always be a set of people who do not know as much as you do in your field, and are willing to learn.

In some cases, the people who are popularly referred to as "experts" may not know how to break concepts down for beginners to easily pick up.

"Experts" are fond of using big words and industry jargon; and so, they end up confusing beginners who are trying to learn the skill.

More often than not, people are looking for people who can break down concepts for them to easily understand.

I remember when I was in the university. Some of my classmates would organise tutorials after our lecturers had taught us, and a lot of people would attend those tutorial classes because they did not fully understand the concepts when the lecturer taught in class, but knew that the tutorial coordinator would break things down for them to understand easily.

The tutorial coordinators were not experts, but at least they could explain what they understood.

This is what I also want you to understand about teaching an online course.

It's not about displaying your breadth of knowledge, but about helping people to learn what you know.

Are you not encouraging quacks?

Anytime I explain this concept to people, they always ask me the following question.

"Are you saying we should all go and start teaching even though we don't know a lot?"

Even though you decide to teach, you can't teach just any topic.

To be able to teach a topic, you should have spent a lot of time developing yourself on that topic, such that you know more than the average person.

If you teach a topic you don't know very well, it might affect your credibility and your ability to make money from online courses.

Nobody knows me

Some other people say, "I'm not an expert, nobody knows me; who will listen to me?"

Here's the thing.

The people who you know as experts, are the people who have positioned themselves as experts.

They have launched information products around the topics they know so well and have taken the time to build a brand. They have built their platforms, shared free content, granted interviews, organised events and many more.

The reason nobody knows you yet is because you have not started doing all of these things.

When you launch your online course, it will force you to launch your personal brand, to build your platform and to share free content. Then, people will start referring to you as the expert.

Do you see the way it works?

Launching your online course helps you to become known as the go-to person for that topic.

If you are completely unknown, the first time you launch your online course, you might get an average of five to ten students, but as you keep growing your brand, your influence will keep growing and your audience size will keep growing. When next you launch your course, more people will pay for it. This is why it's important to have a long term perspective as you launch your course. It is not a get-rich-quick scheme, however as you keep relaunching your online course from time to time as your brand, influence and audience size grows, more people will keep paying for it as long as it solves a problem that they have.

A lot of people who are building their brand and sharing free content online struggle to remain consistent because it's just something they are doing as a hobby. They work on it when they have time, and abandon it when they get busy with other things. On the other hand, when your online activities are tied towards launching a product, it forces you to remain consistent and with consistency comes great rewards.

Give yourself permission

If you are still struggling with the idea of teaching what you know, maybe it's time to give yourself the permission to teach.
I was listening to a friend tell me the story of how she got into a new career path.

She said her boss just walked up to her, gave her a new role and told her to do it.

She tried to protest, "I've never done this before Ma, I'm not sure I can do it..." and her boss told her, "If you don't do it, I'll have to let you go".

This made her to sit up and she started researching on how to complete the task. Today, she has built a career in that new field.
She did it because someone asked her to do it.

Not all of us will get threatened by a boss or receive a push from someone else. Some of us would just have to say to ourselves, "I give myself permission to try this new thing even though I have never done it before".

I'm sure you've noticed, this is not just an ideology that applies to online courses alone. You can literally use it for any goal you want to embark on.

Just say it out loud, "I give myself the permission to launch my online course".

How does that feel?

Reflections

There was another famous person in the bible who also said, "Who am I to do this?"

His name was Moses.

Just think about it, God appeared to him in a burning bush that was not really burning. How miraculous was that?

Out of that burning bush, He said to him:

"I have certainly seen the oppression of my people in Egypt. I have heard their cries of distress because of their harsh slave drivers. Yes, I am aware of their suffering. So I have come down to rescue them from the power of the Egyptians and lead them out of Egypt into their own fertile and spacious land. It is a land flowing with milk and honey—the land where the Canaanites, Hittites, Amorites, Perizzites, Hivites, and Jebusites now live.

Look! The cry of the people of Israel has reached me, and I have seen how harshly the Egyptians abuse them. Now go, for I am sending you to Pharaoh. You must lead my people Israel out of Egypt." - *Exodus 3:7-10 (NLT)*

Moses' first response was:

"Who am I to appear before Pharaoh? Who am I to lead the people of Israel out of Egypt?" - Exodus 3:11 (NLT)

God answered,

"I will be with you. And this is your sign that I am the one who has sent you: When you have brought the people out of Egypt, you will worship God at this very mountain." - *Exodus 3:12 (NLT)*

Can I tell you something?

God is interested in this online course you are thinking about launching.

He will be with you.

It's probably Him who has put this desire in your heart to impact lives.

He's sending you to His people because they have been suffering for lack of knowledge. He wants to take them to their land flowing with milk and honey but He needs someone to show them how.

He's calling you; please stop saying "who am I?"

Just answer the call.

Success Story

"So far more than 20 people have signed up for the course and are learning how to land a job they love through Linkedin."

I knew I wanted to help people get jobs, live life and enjoy their lives but I did not know where to start from.

I signed up for the Course Launched Delivered online course and developed The Linkedin Profile Makeover Course which helps people land their dream jobs on LinkedIn.

So far more than 20 people have signed up for the course and are learning how to land a job they love through Linkedin.

Steph is every girl boss' best friend, an achiever and a wonderful coach. She helped me to believe more in myself more than ever before, and constantly pushes me to be better.

Thank you Stephanie for showing me the light.

You are the best!

Funmilola Kehinde
Founder,CareerswithFunmi

With the Linked in Makeover Course

Your dream job is a click away

visit www.careerswithfunmi.com/shop
To sign up

I'M NOT A TECHIE

An online course is first of all a course.

It is your knowledge that has been packaged in form of a training product.

Just the way you can write a book without being a publisher, you can create a course without being a technology whiz kid.

The most important thing here is your content.

When it comes to the technology aspect, there are basically two approaches you can take.

You either learn how to do it yourself, or you can hire it out.

Technology has even become quite advanced. We now have a lot of tools and platforms that are very easy to use.

When I was studying Computer Science in the university, I had to learn how to write different programming languages, and it looked as if the only way to build a career in tech was to be a programming guru.

Now, you don't even have to touch a line of code to build a website.

As long as you can use a phone or a laptop, you can launch an online course by the click of a button.

Who is a Techie?

The tech aspect of launching an online course only feels overwhelming when you don't know how to what to do, but you can actually learn it.

I have grandmothers who have worked with me to launch their online courses and today, they are managing their platforms by themselves.

Anytime I hear people say, "I'm not a techie ", I laugh and say, "What is the definition of a techie?"

We usually refer to people who know how to use tech tools as techies.

The interesting thing is, nobody came into this world knowing how to use any tech tool. We have learnt everything that we know on earth.
The "techie people" as we call them have just learnt how to use tech tools. If you also decide to learn how to use these tools, you will also become techie.

Tech is too complicated

The next argument is, "I really want to learn how to use technology but it sounds so complicated".

The big question is, "Who are you learning from?"

Are you learning from someone who has taken the time to break it down so that a beginner like you can grasp the skills or are you learning from someone who can only speak using tech jargon?

If you learn from a teacher, who has taken the time to explain all the steps in an easy-to-follow manner, it will be so easy for you to learn and to implement.

Anything whatsoever can be taught.

It's not dependent on the type of person you are, your background, what you studied in the university, what country you live in and so on; it's all a function of how open you are to learning new things.

Once upon a time, there was no such thing as Facebook.

We all learnt how to use Facebook.
Once upon a time, there was no such thing as WhatsApp.
We all learnt how to use it too.

The people who have not learnt how to use these platforms yet, are standing by the sidelines and saying things like, "I'm not a techie".

What they are really saying is, "I'm not interested in learning how to use it" because as far as the human mind is concerned, there is nothing that you cannot learn.

Tech is Expensive

There is no better time to launch your online course because there are now so many easy-to-use tools as well as a lot of affordable options.

I dare say that there is an option for every budget.

For instance, if you want to record video lessons for your online course, you can hire a videographer, you can just record yourself with your mobile phone or you can even record yourself speaking over a PowerPoint presentation.

If you want to have your own online school, you can buy an already designed online school, or you can just open an account on a platform like Teachable or Thinkific. You will get an online school immediately and you will only need to pay a monthly fee to host your online course on the platform.

You can even receive payments from your online course from any country in the world. When I started selling online courses, there was no platform that would allow me to receive payments from other countries because I live in Nigeria. I had to tell my foreign clients to make payments to me using Western Union. Today, there are platforms that help me to easily receive money from all over the world, and people can pay for my online courses with just the click of a button.

Things have really gotten easier and they are going to get much easier. That being said, I want to also point this out. When you use technology, there are going to be times that it just does not work. Links might get broken, forms might stop working, your website might refuse to load and everything that can go wrong may go wrong. When things go wrong, please don't lift up your hands and say "I'm done with technology".

Every problem can be fixed. Every problem has a plan B.

A Tech Mindset

It is your attitude around technology that is more important, and this attitude is a choice. You can decide how you want to feel about a situation.

It is your attitude around technology that is more important, and this attitude is a choice.
You can decide how you want to feel about a situation.

When it seems like all hell has broken loose, focus on your why. Why are you launching this online course? What will happen after this online course has been launched? How will the lives of your students be changed after you launch your online course?

As you learn how to use technology, this is what will keep you going as you deal with the challenges that come up, and in the event that you decide to outsource the tech aspect, this is what will keep you going as you make that investment.

All hell won't break loose. You can launch your course without hitches, but even if there are challenges, please don't lose sight of what's really important.

Reflections

Tech can be challenging for a lot of people, but every assignment comes with its own share of challenges.

Whenever we hear from God and we know that God is calling us to take on an assignment, we tend to believe that there won't be challenges.

When God was sending out Moses to lead the people of Israel out of Egypt, He said to him,

"But I know that the king of Egypt will not let you go unless a mighty hand forces him." - **Exodus 3:19 (NLT)**

God already knows that there will be challenges.

At some point, He even said to Moses,

"But I will harden Pharaoh's heart, and though I multiply my signs and wonders in Egypt, he will not listen to you." - **Exodus 7:3 (NIV)**

When you face challenges on your assignment, it does not mean that God is no longer with you.

He's still with you, but every challenge you are going through has a purpose.

It could be that God wants to teach you something.
It could be that God wants to make you a lot more compassionate.
It could be that God wants to make you a stronger person.
It could be that God wants to equip you for a bigger assignment.
It could also be that God wants to show the world that He is God, just like He did with the Egyptians.

He said to Moses,

"But I will harden Pharaoh's heart, and though I multiply my signs and wonders in Egypt, he will not listen to you. Then I will lay my hand on Egypt and with mighty acts of judgment I will bring out my divisions, my people the Israelites. And the Egyptians will know that I am the Lord when I stretch out my hand against Egypt and bring the Israelites out of it." - **Exodus 7:3-5 (NIV)**

Don't abandon your assignment because of the challenges.

There's always a way out.

Success Story

"Today, I have about 26 students from different countries of the world taking my online courses."

I enrolled into the Course Launched Delivered Online Course even though I did not know anything about technology except how to operate my phone and laptop. It wasn't easy at first but Steph was always there to explain, clarify things and show me the way forward. Even though I didn't have all I needed (like a website, a standard kitchen, a course topic, email list and so on), I successfully created my first online course called "Your First 7 Cakes".

With all I learnt from Course Launch Delivered, I launched my online course with an email list of just 600 and about 400 Instagram followers. I made sure I did everything Steph taught in the course and I got a total of 9 students which is a record breaker for someone with such a lean email list.

In Course Launched Delivered, I learnt how to host a webinar, how to create a converting launch plan, how to create a know-like-trust synergy with my audience, how to define my niche in a saturated industry etc. I learnt how to be me! Stephanie Obi gave me a voice! I knew I had a talent but Steph refined and polished my talent to become very profitable!

After two months, I launched my course again at a higher price (about 20% increase). Today, I have about 26 students from different countries of the world taking my online courses. I have developed a total of 6 more online courses, some of which I am planning to launch soon.

I now prefer to take more students through my online course because it's less stressful than delivering physical classes.

Believe it or not, Stephanie Obi is a game changer!

Love you Steph!
Miriam
www.bakeandbeadsacademy.com

YOUR FIRST
7
CAKES
Online Course

What you will learn:
Madeira Cake
Rich Fruit Cake
Red Velvet Cake
Vanilla Cream Cake
Classic Sponge Cake
Rich Chocolate Cake
Classic Carrot Cake
Buttercream Cake Decoration

With Bonuses!

Instructor:
Miriam
MaeRaymond
(Bake and Beads)

Nine

I'M NOT SURE ANYBODY WILL PAY FOR MY COURSE

One reason a number of people make this comment is that we all have a habit of taking what we know for granted.

It comes to us so easily that we don't imagine that anybody will pay to learn this skill that now comes so naturally to us.

There's no one person on earth who knows everything.

The things that come easily to you, might not come easily to another person. We all have different experiences that have shaped the skills we now have, and that is why we all have different strengths.
Your job is to find the people who want to learn this topic that you know so well, and that's where marketing online comes in.

The internet has even made this very easy because you are no longer restricted to only the people who live within your local community.

If the people who live in your city are not interested in learning your skill, there are people living all over the world who are interested in learning it.

When I launched my first online course on Ankara accessories, there were a lot of other people organizing live workshops on the same topic in the city I live in, so the competition was intense. My competitors were slashing prices to attract more customers.

I marketed online and I started finding people in other cities all across the country and even outside the country who were looking for someone to teach them how to make Ankara accessories, and they were so excited to find me.

They didn't have to travel to my city or to pay for hotel accommodation; they could just log on to my online course and watch the lessons from wherever they were.

The world became my marketplace.

Why Do People Pay for Things?

Another reason some people worry about whether anyone would pay for their online course is because the information they want to teach is already available for free online and they wonder why anyone would pay for it.

People pay for online courses because they are looking for solutions to their problems, not information. If you package your online course as a solution to a pressing problem, then the people who need that solution will pay for it.

There will always be a set of people in any given industry, who want answers to their questions and are willing to pay someone who has done all the research, made all the mistakes, experimented, and has got results to show them how to also get results in an organised, step-by-step manner.

There will always be a set of people in any given industry,
who want answers to their questions and are willing to pay someone who
has done all the research, made all the mistakes, experimented, and
gotten results to show them
how to get results in an organised step-by-step manner.

They don't want to spend their entire time on Google, figuring things out by themselves. They have so much to do, and they will happily pay someone who can give them a proven and organised way of getting results, organised, and presented by a brand that they can emotionally connect with.

For instance, I laugh, sing silly songs and crack funny jokes while I'm delivering my content in my online courses. People like the way I teach and will gladly pay for my courses because I make it feel like fun, and I help them get results in a much shorter time. This is a solution.

I've identified several things that people happily pay for.

People will pay for anything that will:

1. Make them more money
2. Help them save money
3. Save them time
4. Help them build stronger relationships
5. Save and secure their lives
6. Make them admired
7. Make them appreciated
8. Make them accepted
9. Help them to relax
10. Make things easier for them
11. Give them an amazing experience

You have a solution, but you have to tie your online course to the results people are in need of.

A clear way to get this right is to ask, "What do people really want and what is stopping them from achieving it? What is their pressing problem?"

If your online course is not addressing a pressing problem, people will not pay for the course because they have other things they have to pay for like their house rent, children's school fees, food, etc.

I once conducted a survey and I asked people,

"Do you agree that vitamin C is good for the body?"

They all answered "yes".

"How many times have you taken vitamin C in the last four weeks?"

Out of all the people I surveyed, only one person had taken vitamin C, and that was because she had a cold.

Many of them said they didn't remember to take vitamin C.

My next question was, "Do you agree that pain relievers can stop headaches?"

They all answered yes.

"If you have a banging headache, does anybody need to remind you to take a pain reliever?"

"Noooooooo", they all answered.

You know why?

When you have a banging headache or a pressing problem that keeps you up at night, nobody has to encourage you to get a solution. You are the one who will search everywhere to look for a solution and when you find it, you will be grateful to the person who provided the solution.

That's the way it works with online courses.

If you package your online course as a solution to someone's problem, they are most likely already looking for you and when they find you, they will not only pay for your online course, they will also sing your praises and thank you profusely for creating the course.

Will People Pay if the Price is High?

Another mindset block I hear all the time is, "I'm not sure anyone will pay for my online course if I set it at this price..."

People pay for things they find valuable.

If an item is very valuable, we generally pay a high price for it.

If an item is not very valuable, we might struggle to pay for it even if it's low priced.

As you package your online course, one thing to be clear about is the value your online course will be delivering for your clients.

If your online course is very valuable, your clients will pay the price you place on the online course because they want that value.

Value is usually relative, but the best way to show the true value of your online course is to put a figure to it.

To calculate the value of your online course, you can ask:

"What will they be able to do after they take the course? What is the monetary value of this?"
"How will their lives change for the better? Will they be able to get an extra stream of income or a promotion or more time with their kids? How much is this worth?

"How much money can they make if they implement what I teach in this course?"

"How much money will they waste if they don't know what I am teaching in this course?"

"Will they be able to replicate the results they will get from my course over and over again? How much will they potentially make if they keep implementing the knowledge?"

"How much will they pay a professional to do what I am teaching in this course?"

"How much will they pay a coach to guide them through what I am teaching in this course?"

"How much will they spend if they had to travel to attend a live workshop?" (Include the cost of transportation, accommodation, etc.)

If you show people the value of your course, vis-a-vis the price of your course, they will happily pay for it, because the price is only a fraction of the true value.

I've also heard people say, "I'm not sure anyone will pay for my online course because it's not focused on helping people make money online". This is another mindset block.

You can make money from online courses in any industry or niche as long as there are a set of people who want to learn that topic, and there are examples of people who are already doing this.

People have launched online courses on tidying houses, parenting, using Microsoft Excel, eating right, losing weight, singing, taking tests, preparing for job interviews, learning a new language, taking care of pets, playing tennis, marriage, raising teenagers, taking photographs and many more!

Reflections

You are not the only one who is worried that nobody would pay attention to you.

Moses also had that concern.

He said to God,

"What if they won't believe me or listen to me? What if they say, 'The Lord never appeared to you'?" **- Exodus 4:1 (NLT)**

Valid question, don't you think?

Then the Lord asked him,

"What is that in your hand?" "A shepherd's staff," Moses replied. "Throw it down on the ground," the Lord told him. So Moses threw down the staff, and it turned into a snake! Moses jumped back.

Then the Lord told him, "Reach out and grab its tail." So Moses reached out and grabbed it, and it turned back into a shepherd's staff in his hand.

"Perform this sign," the Lord told him. "Then they will believe that the Lord, the God of their ancestors—the God of Abraham, the God of Isaac, and the God of Jacob—really has appeared to you." **- Exodus 4:2-5 (NLT)**

My favourite part of God's response is this line,

"What is that in your hand?"

God always uses what you have, to show other people that He has sent you.

You can use the knowledge you have in your head to help people see signs and wonders in their lives.

Moses was holding a mere shepherd's staff. It was just a simple wooden rod. This is probably a rod he carved out of some wood from a tree, but it was good enough for God to use to perform signs and wonders.

Don't despise your gift.
Don't despise what you have.
God wants to use it to do so much more.

Success Story

"Today, I have about 26 students from different countries of the world taking my online courses."

I took the Course Launched Delivered online course in 2017 and I was not disappointed. When I launched my course in January, I was scared but I did it afraid.

When the first student paid, I honestly could not believe it. I thought "Wow! Someone actually paid for my course!". That feeling got better as I received more payment alerts.

I launched my online course, "Track Your Profit" which is an online bookkeeping course that helps small business owners to manage their finances better.

I even learnt more than how to launch a course. I learnt how to connect in the social media space and how to build a website which I did all by myself. I made very valuable connections and more importantly, I made sales.

Stephanie is a great teacher and I am happy I learnt this from her.

Basirat Razaq-Shuaib
http://actifylimited.com/

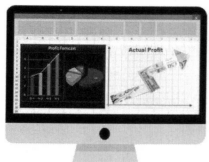

I'M NOT REALLY SURE OF WHAT I'M DOING

If you feel this way, you are not alone. It's very common with people who are trying to launch their online courses for the first time.

Even though they have achieved a lot and can easily teach, they start getting thoughts like:

"I feel like a fraud"

"People are going to find out that I'm a fraud and my name will be ruined"

"I didn't really deserve all I achieved; I just got lucky. How can I then teach?"

"I'm not sure my course will help anyone; I'm so scared of people putting up bad reviews of my course on social media..."

These thoughts are so dangerous because they encourage fear and anxiety. Before you know it, you will find yourself procrastinating, losing confidence, keeping quiet and shying away from any form of attention, etc.

You'll end up sabotaging and talking yourself out of launching your online course.

There is a well-researched phenomenon called the Imposter Syndrome common among successful people. It is the inability to internalize accomplishments such as academic excellence, recognition, promotions, etc. Successful women would typically attribute their success to things like luck, perseverance, their parents, their friends, their network, being in the right place at the right time, a government policy etc.

This makes them to live with a perpetual fear that one day, people are going to find out that they should not have achieved what they have achieved and call them frauds.

The funny part is, these are the people who are more than qualified to teach because they have actually achieved something.

If you find that you have the imposter syndrome, one of the reasons why you feel like a fraud is because you have not actually owned your accomplishments.

Please believe me when I say this:

You deserve everything you have achieved and there are many people out there who would love to learn from you.

Own it!

Look at yourself in the mirror and say out loud:

"I am smart"
"I am talented"
"I am strong"
"I am confident"
"I am beautiful"
"I am enough"

If you want to stop feeling like an imposter, you have to stop thinking like one.

The people who do not feel like imposters are not any better than the people who feel like imposters. They just have different thoughts.

You can change the way you feel by changing the way you think.

---

*You can change the way you
feel by changing the way you think.*

Instead of thinking, "I have no idea what I am doing"; you can think, "This is a new experience for me. I'm going to learn so much as I launch my first online course."

Instead of thinking, "People are going to find out that I'm a fraud and my name will be ruined"; you can think, "I am smart, I know so much already, I am enough."

Instead of thinking, "I'm not sure my course will help anyone; I'm so scared of people putting up bad reviews of my course on social media..."; you can think, "There are so many people who don't know half of the things I know. If I can just help those set of people, they will sing my praise on social media."

At first, it might feel like your mind is a battleground.

The mindset blocks will come to speak to you, but you have to fight back with your positive thoughts.

Just keep at it.

If you keep saying your positive thoughts out loud, your thoughts will lead to actions, and you will find yourself launching your course.

Fight

I call this period "war", because that's what it is.

If you don't fight for your self worth, you are going to keep on sabotaging yourself and you will see other people who are not as qualified as you are launching their own online courses, making money, impacting lives, speaking about their students' testimonials and you will feel bad because you know that you are more qualified, but you just allowed mindset blocks to hold you back.

Sometimes it helps to speak to someone you trust who can help you put things in perspective. People who experience the imposter syndrome are usually scared of voicing it out so that they don't hear things like, "Yes I agree, I always suspected that you were not that good.'

I also experienced my own share of imposter syndrome before I launched my signature online course, "Course Launched Delivered" which helps people to create, launch and deliver online courses. I confided in a friend, and I said to her, "I don't think I'm good enough to teach this course".

She looked at me in shock and said, "How can you say that when I come to you for advice on online courses? You have launched over twenty online courses when people are still struggling to launch one".

This statement brought me back to my senses and made me start questioning why I was doubting myself.

I went ahead to launch that online course and the "thank you" messages I have been receiving are unbelievable. All these would not have happened if I listened to the mindset blocks in my head, telling me rubbish.

Reflections

Moses also felt like a fraud.

He didn't feel like he was equipped to lead the people of Israel out of Egypt.

He kept pushing back:

"Who am I to appear before Pharaoh? Who am I to lead the people of Israel out of Egypt?" – **Exodus 3:11 (NLT)**

He was scared that people would call him a fraud.

"What if they won't believe me or listen to me? What if they say, 'The Lord never appeared to you'?" – **Exodus 4:1 (NLT)**

How he felt did not change the fact that God called him.

In fact, if you look at the circumstances surrounding Moses' birth, you would notice that God had separated him for His work from the beginning. Moses was born at a time when the Pharaoh of Egypt had given an instruction that every newborn Hebrew boy must be thrown into the Nile River.

When his mother gave birth to him, she saw that he was a special baby and kept him hidden for three months. When she could no longer hide him, she put him in a basket and laid him along the bank of the Nile River.

Pharaoh's daughter discovered him and she later adopted him as one of her own sons. Moses was probably the only Hebrew boy his age that was alive at the time. God had preserved his life because he had a special assignment, and yet when it was time to execute the assignment, he didn't feel that God could use him.

How you feel is not an indicator of whether God can use you or not.

Before God formed you in the womb, He knew you. Before you were born, He set you apart. He appointed you as a prophet to the nations according to Jeremiah 1 verse 5.

Your life has a purpose that is bigger than your feelings.

Think about this and let it change the way you think about yourself.

If you change your thoughts, your feelings will change.

Eleven

I DON'T HAVE TIME

It does take time to create an online course, especially since you will be creating an asset that can make you money for the rest of your life.

If the time required to set it all up is what's stopping you from getting started, what you are really saying is:

"It's not yet a priority for me".

When it becomes a priority, you will create the time for it and you will find a way to stay committed.

What Is in It for You?

A great way to remain committed to creating an online course is to always remember what is at stake.

I know that your online course will impact the lives of so many people, but how will it change your own life?

For some people, an online course could help you create more time to play with your kids because you don't have to work one-on-one with all your clients. For some others, it could be making more money to invest in a personal project or taking your kids on a vacation. It might even be about finally being able to quit your 9 to 5.

Whatever the case might be, you have to always remember why you are creating this online course.

If there's no personal reason why you want to launch your online course, you might struggle with procrastination.

Set a Goal

When you get clear on your why, it helps to set a goal that will keep you focused.

When exactly will you launch your online course?

It also helps to be realistic about this goal.

Think about the challenges that might stop you from achieving your goal and come with solutions to overcome these challenges.

You might need to get the support of your spouse as you go on this journey.

You might need to get the support of a coach as you go on this journey.

You might need to wake up one hour earlier to work on your course.

Whatever the situation is for you, take ownership of this project. It is your life that will change once you have a successful online course.

Vision Board

It also helps to put up images of what your life will be like after you launch your online course on a vision board.

A vision board is a board you can create, that will include images and texts that represent where you want to be in the future.

Vision boards work because they help you to keep your goals and dreams top of mind, and each time you are reminded of your goals, your subconscious mind will keep looking for ways to move you closer to achieving them. Your mind will begin to notice the available resources you have that you might have been ignoring, the right people who can help you, and the opportunities you can take advantage of to achieve your goals.

This is why I always recommend that you create a vision board and hang it up in a place where you can see it everyday.

Some people hang their vision boards on a wall in their bedrooms, some make it small, so that they can keep it on a photo frame on their desks, while others hang it in their bathroom. You can keep your vision board anywhere, as long as you look at it everyday.

To create your vision board, you need to:

1. **Write a list**
   Write down a list of what your life will look like after you create your online course. It helps to do this exercise when you are not stressed or in a hurry to go somewhere. You can put on some music to relax your nerves and just dream.

2. **Get your images**
   Look through several magazines to find pictures that represent what you wrote down on your list. Cut the images from the magazine. You can also check online to get some images. Print out the images from your computer.

3. **Paste the images on a board**
   You can use any board at all – cardboard, corkboard or a wooden board. Just use whatever you can easily lay your hands on. Arrange your cut up images on the board and paste them using glue or push pins.

4. **Hang your board up**
   This is the most important step in the process. You have to hang your board up in a place where you will see it everyday. Whatever you focus on, grows.

Accountability Partners

Having some form of accountability works wonders.

I wish I could explain how motivated my clients are when they see other people in the programme working towards their online course goals.

If they were giving themselves excuses before then, they wake up.

When you have someone who is working with you on a goal, it's difficult to keep coming back to the person with excuses about why you've not done what you said you would do.

It also helps to have people that you can share your struggles with, who will also tell you about how they dealt with the same issues you are struggling with and overcame them.

You also need people who can be honest with you and give you constructive feedback or new ideas that you have not considered previously.

Personalised Schedule

Another way to remain committed to creating your online course even if you don't have time is to design a schedule that works for you.

Comparison is the thief of joy. If you compare yourself to your friend who has more time on her hands and can pump out her online course in days, you are going to feel very depressed.

Instead of looking on the outside, look at your own calendar. What is your life like? When can you fit in the time to work on your online course?

There might never be a time when you are not as busy as you are now, so you have to find a way of working with the cards you have been dealt.

When I created my first online course, I was still engaged in a 9 to 5.

I decided to take time off work to create my course content. I went on leave, and I made the most of my time.

Now that I work for myself full time, I still have a lot of things fighting for my attention, and so I spread my to-dos over a 3-month period.

I dedicate two to four hours per week to working on my course, and I spend the rest of my time, attending to the other things that need my attention.

This keeps me focused.

There's really no right or wrong answer; you just have to find a method that works for you.

Some people have outsourced some of the tasks so that they don't have to do everything themselves.

Some people have invested in some tools so that they don't have to spend a lot of time on some tasks.

Some people have decided to track how they were spending their time, to find pockets of time that they could spend on creating their course instead.

Some people have gone away on a 2-week retreat all by themselves, to a place where they can focus on their online course.

There are so many options, because where there's a will, there's always a way.

You just have to remember why you want to create a course in the first place and your mind will come up with a way if you want it badly enough.

Twelve

I AM CAMERA SHY

I can relate with this because I was an extremely shy person.

I could never do anything that would bring attention to myself.

When I was in secondary school, my name was once announced at the assembly ground as one of the people who performed very well academically and they wanted to award me with a gift.

I heard my name but I could not get myself to walk up to the podium because I was shy.

The people around me were nudging me, "Go on now, Go now...", but I could not move.

I just stood there and watched as they gave gifts to other people on the list.

This is what happens to people who are shy.

You watch other people get opportunities but you take no action because you are scared of putting yourself out there.

I used to say, "This is how I am", but after I lost another incredible opportunity, I started to say to myself, "I cannot continue like this".

Today, nobody believes me when I say I used to be shy because I've changed so much.

Nobody was born shy.

There are certain things that must have happened to you in the past that made you become shy.

Maybe when you were 5 years old, you danced in a party and the other kids laughed at your dance steps.

Your brain began to believe that if you did anything in public, people would laugh at you.

This mindset has remained with you for so long and is now manifesting as "I'm camera shy".

Fear of Rejection

The first step to overcome this feeling is to address the reason you don't feel comfortable with putting yourself out there.

Why are you afraid of being on camera?
One common reason is the fear of rejection.
What if they don't listen to me?
What if they don't like my posts?
What if they criticize what I'm saying?
What if they choose another person over me?
It hurts, I know.

But, I want you to ask yourself this question:

"What is the worst thing that can happen to me?

Think about it deeply.

People will not like your posts...so what? Does that kill?

Rejection really cannot be avoided, as there's no way everybody can like you. Not everybody will like your posts or even understand what you are about.

This is because it's not everybody who needs you. However, there are a set of people who need your help and are desperately looking for a solution to their problems.

When you put yourself out there, you make it easy for the people who need you to find you.

Fear of What People Will Say

Another concern is the fear of what people will say.

What if they laugh at me?

What if they judge me?

What if they say, "Everybody is creating online courses, you too, you want to create an online course. Follow-follow!"

Once again, it's okay to get these type of comments, as everybody is entitled to their opinions.

Remember why you want to teach and focus on that.

Remember who you want to help and focus on that.

Remember how lives will be impacted and focus on that.
I've seen people come on social media to address the people who are laughing at them or judging them, commonly referred to as "haters".

This is a waste of your time as it shows that you are focusing on your haters and what they said to you or sometimes it might even be what you imagine they are saying about you.

Whatever you focus on grows.

Focusing on your haters will only attract more haters.

Instead of feeling like the whole world is against you, practise feeling like people want you to succeed and they are cheering you on.

When you are about to go on camera, imagine that people are watching your videos with smiles on their faces.

Imagine that people are listening to you and writing you thank-you notes for recording that video.

Imagine that people are watching you on video and are spreading good messages about you.

As you focus on these good thoughts, this is what you will attract into your life. This exercise will also help you to get comfortable about getting on camera, because you expect that people will be watching you and saying thank you.

Like I always say, this is war.
There are many times you will come on video and think, "Oh, I didn't do this thing right" or "I should have done it this way".

If you focus on all the things you did wrong, you will not be encouraged to share that video, and that will defeat the purpose.

Instead of focusing on all the things that went wrong, think about the things that went right and congratulate yourself on those things.

Give yourself a pat on the back.

Clap for yourself.

Sometimes, you have to be your best cheerleader because you won't always be surrounded by people who can cheer you on.

How to Prepare for the Camera

I remember the first time I got on camera to do a video shoot.

It felt very awkward speaking to a camera.

I quickly rushed through my script because I wanted to get it over and done with.

Of course, we had to re-shoot the video and with time, I learnt how to prepare to get in front of the camera.

I start by asking myself, "How do I want people to feel after watching this video?"

If I want them to feel happy, I try to get myself in a happy state. I sing. I play some happy music. I dance. In no time, I'm happy, laughing and cheerful.

When I get in front of the camera in that state, joy is bubbling out of every part of my body.

I also prepare a script or some bullet points so that I remember what I want to say. This helps me to act and look confident because I have an agenda and I'm prepared to speak about the points I have prepared.

As I look at the camera, I picture the image of the person who needs my help and I speak to the camera as if I'm speaking to that person in real life.

If you prepare for your videos like this, they will always come out well.
I get asked this question. "Do I always need to wear make-up when I want to come on camera?"

It's a good idea to make an effort to look good when you come on video because people make an impression about you within the first seven seconds of meeting you, and that includes meeting you over video.

Make an attempt to look neat.

If you however find that you are not taking the plunge to go on camera because the thought of applying make-up discourages you, don't bother with the make-up.

Comb your hair, look neat and go live without make-up. Don't let make-up become your excuse.

Don't let anything become an excuse; this is war and you must win.

Reflections

There were no cameras during Moses' time on earth, but he was also worried about getting in front of people.

Once again, Moses protested,
"If I go to the people of Israel and tell them, 'The God of your ancestors has sent me to you,' they will ask me, 'What is his name?' Then what should I tell them?"
– Exodus 3:13 (NLT)

God replied to Moses,

"I AM WHO I AM. Say this to the people of Israel: I AM has sent me to you."
God also said to Moses, "Say this to the people of Israel:
Yahweh, the God of your ancestors—the God of Abraham,
the God of Isaac, and the God of Jacob—has sent me to you.
This is my eternal name, my name to remember for all generations.
– Exodus 3:14-15 (NLT)

When you have to speak in front of people, it's quite easy to become self-conscious.

What will I say? Am I even making sense?

When you feel that way, focus on the message that God has laid in your heart. When you focus on this message, it won't be about what people will say or how you look; instead, it will be about the lives that should be impacted by your message.

Success Story

"Today, I have about 26 students from different countries of the world taking my online courses."

I had a huge fear about showing myself to the world, and yet this is a key element in connecting with this same world.

Course Launched Delivered showed me, guided me and encouraged me to show up and to stop hiding.

Having classmates with similar fears helped us to work the fears out of ourselves hand-in-hand. It was also comforting to hear Steph talk about her 'crushed' fears of becoming visible even though she was still an introvert.

Steph, my classmates and the Course Launched Delivered content explained that going live, showing my photos and telling my story would enable me connect better with people but also help more people connect with me, receive my message and buy from me.

The hiding was over. I came out.

I started working on my website, defining my message and offering.

Course Launched Delivered has given me many tools beyond just how to create an online course. It is truly transformational.

In hindsight, I wanted more than just creating an online course. I wanted to be given direction - on my niche, on what products to create and how to take my business forward online being that I am a full time stay-at-home mum. I also wanted to overcome 2 major fears - showing myself to the world and charging a fee as I do so much for free.

Course Launched Delivered did this and more.

Apart from this, I went ahead to organise a book reading event for my daughter with the plan to monetize her book in future. The Course Launched Delivered effect!

Miriam Elegbede
www.miriamelegbede.com

I JUST WANT TO HELP PEOPLE, I DON'T WANT TO MAKE MONEY

This is another strong limiting belief that stops people from turning their knowledge into profit.

I've found that a lot of us are not comfortable with the idea of making money, even though we say that we want to make more money.

The idea of creating a product and putting a price on it makes us feel like we are being greedy.

There is this intense feeling of shame that people with this mindset block have at the thought of turning the knowledge they have into a product.

They say things like:

"It will look as if I'm begging people to buy from me. I don't want to beg anybody, it's better I give it out for free".

"The people I want to help can't pay me; they are suffering. I just want to give it to them for free".

"Everything is not about money".

"Why should I be making money from this, when people are out there suffering?"

"I'm not really a business person".

These are money blocks.

Money blocks are excuses you tell yourself that stop you from making more money. Many times, we are not even aware of them, but they are dictating what actions we take and don't take.

They are based on beliefs we have come to accept about money, that we may have picked up during our childhood, from our environment, past experiences, etc.

Consider this money block: "I just want to help people, I don't want to make money".
This money block is based on the belief that you can't help people and make money too. This belief is flawed.

If you package your knowledge as an online course, you will be giving people a step-by-step guide to help them achieve a result, and you will be helping them in the process because these people have been looking for a solution to their problems and have not yet found someone who can bring them a solution in a way that they can understand and implement.

If you want to keep teaching for free, that's fine but the truth of the matter is that, many of the people you want to help will not have access to your free sessions. When you teach for free, there is usually a limit to your impact.

You are limited by time, because you are not always available to give free sessions.
You are limited by the number of people you can impact, because there are so many people living in different cities of the world, and they cannot attend the free sessions you give in the city where you live.

You will find that it's difficult to scale up your capacity to help this way.

On one hand, it's going to become too expensive to keep hosting your free sessions as the number of people you want to help keep increasing, and you might eventually stop because you can no longer afford it. On the other hand, you may find that you don't have time to keep helping people for free, because you are spending most of your time doing the things that bring you money.

In some other cases, you might discover different ways to help people and you just may not be able to afford it. For instance, if you give people business advice and you see that the people you are helping need some form of capital, wanting to create a fund that can offer small loans to the entrepreneurs is great but that idea needs to be funded from somewhere.

Impacting lives costs money and if there's no way to fund it, it becomes unsustainable. If you really want to help people, you have to find a sustainable way of doing it that can also be scaled up, and that's where online courses can come in.

I Want to Give Out My Course for Free

There's also the thought, "Why can't I launch an online course and give it out for free?"

You can, but the danger is that people usually don't value what they get for free.

I've given my friends access to my online courses for free, and they never logged in.

Not because they didn't need it; they just didn't value it.

People value what they pay for. If they had to sacrifice the money they would have used for something else to pay for my online course, they would have taken the course very seriously.

I've found that the people who get the best results from my online course are people who took the biggest risks. They watched every lesson, completed every assignment because they desperately wanted results and were not planning on taking chances.

So, in a way, you are not really helping people by giving things to them for free.

If they can't afford your course in one go, you can create installment plans for them.

If you are trying to help people who really can't afford your course, you can reduce the price of your course, but they have to pay something so that they can take it seriously.

The process of launching an online course even involves giving out a lot of free high quality content. If you give out free content, you should not feel bad that people can't afford your course. A lot of people have made money by just implementing the advice I gave out in my free content.

I Feel Ashamed

Let's talk about the issue of shame, "It will look as if I'm begging people to buy from me, I don't want to beg anybody. It's better I give it out for free".

When you create an online course, you have created a solution to a problem that some people have.

When the people who need this solution find you selling your online course, do you think that they look at you and say, "Look at this person begging me to solve my problem?"

Not quite.

The only people you will have to beg to buy your products are the people who are not your ideal clients. They don't have a problem to solve, they don't see why they should buy your product and they may pay for your online course because they want to support you but they don't really need your course.

If you focus on finding the people who are actually struggling because they have not come in contact with your online course, they will thank you profusely after they pay for your online course.

Is it possible to feel ashamed of creating a product that changes lives?

Not at all.

You should feel pride instead.

If you find yourself feeling ashamed because you are selling an online course, you are probably not focusing on the lives you can impact with your course. You are most likely worried about what people will say about you and you really can't live your life based on the expectations of others because you can't please everybody.

No matter what you do or what your intentions are, there will always be a set of people who will say hurtful things about you.

Most people project their own mindset blocks about money on others. They try to make you look bad by saying things like, "Should you not do this for free? How can you be charging for it?"

They don't understand the value of getting people to pay for value and they are also dealing with their own money blocks. Be patient with them, and don't take their words to heart.

So many people have left jobs they were not very passionate about, to dedicate to a life of teaching others through online courses, masterclasses, books, coaching, etc. If they were not getting paid for the value they were giving out, they would not have been able to do this full-time. They would have still been stuck with helping people for free only during the weekends or when they could find the time. The big question is, how many people can you really help that way?

You are giving out value and you deserve to be paid for it.

The price people pay for your course is nothing compared to the actual value people can get from your course.

*The price people pay for your course
is nothing compared to the actual value
people can get from your course.*

Can you place a price on a saved marriage, having kids that turn out well-adjusted, becoming financially independent, becoming more visible at the workplace, overcoming depression or launching a dream business?

These and more are the type of benefits people get from taking online courses. Take pride in the fact that you are changing lives.

Success Story

*"I have created, launched and delivered my course.
I feel like there's nothing I can't do."*

I enrolled for Course Launched Delivered online course at a time when I was at crossroads in my life.

The limiting belief I had at the time was that I run a social enterprise and so, I shouldn't charge worth for the invaluable time and resources I was giving people; it was a major dilemma for me.

I was afraid to make the investment and unsure of what the outcome would be.

However, I took the leap and I went from having very little knowledge about online courses to creating a mid-range transformational course that people paid for within the first 48 hours of my launch.

For me, the course was so much more than just creating an extra source of income or monetizing my knowledge. It was about beliefs that had held me back from truly doing things afraid, charting new paths and living life fully.

I realized that I am full of worth.

I realized that I am valuable and there is nothing wrong in charging for the service I render.

That is my major testimony.
I have created, launched and delivered my course. I feel like there's nothing I can't do.

So, I'm going to do it again.

The knowledge I gained from the course has helped me write compelling sales pages, proposals, give presentations, understand the psychology of marketing and so much more.

The techie part of it was so invaluable!

To sum it up, my students have incredible and teary-eyed testimonials of my course that validate not just the hard work, but my life's purpose.

Hauwa Ojeifo
www.shewriteswoman.org

I'M NOT GOOD ENOUGH

This thought is usually disguised by statements such as "I won't launch my online course until I get a certification".

This is born of a belief that it is certification that can make you credible.

People are looking for people with results, not certifications. Granted, there are a few topics where people will demand to see a qualification before they can listen to you, for instance, health related topics.

Other than that, you really don't need a certification to teach. People just want to see that you can help them to get results.
For instance, I started my online course journey by teaching people how to make Ankara accessories. What certification did I need to have to do that? None.

What was more important was that I actually knew how to make the accessories, and I had proof of the accessories I had made.

Don't get me wrong; certifications are great, because you learn more things in the process of acquiring them but not having them should not stop you from creating an online course.

What you already know is enough to get started.

I'm not Pretty Enough

Another way people stop themselves from launching online courses is by saying to themselves, "I'm not pretty enough, I can't put my face out there".

This is particularly painful, as I have seen people who don't feel they are pretty or handsome enough stop themselves from sharing their gifts with the world.

They struggle with getting in front of a camera, sharing a video or even posting their pictures on the internet.

They are constantly worried about what people will say about their looks and even when other people tell them that they are pretty, they don't believe them.

If you want to launch an online course but you are scared of putting your face out there because you secretly feel that you are not pretty enough, the reason you believe this is because someone told you that you are not pretty and you believed it.

Please allow me to change that narrative for you.

You are pretty, beautiful and wonderfully made.

If you are a man, you are handsome.

You are enough.

People like you just the way you are.

When the people you have been sent to listen to you, they are not going to be having long meetings about your face or what you look like. Instead they are going to talk about how you impacted their lives, so let's focus on what really matters - impacting lives.

The more you focus on how many lives your course will impact, the more comfortable you will feel about putting your face out there, because you will realise that it's not about you.

When you keep focusing on how you look, how your hair looks, the clothes you have, how your voice sounds and so on, you might find that you're holding yourself back.

However, when you focus on the woman who can save her marriage because she took your online course or the man who can now pay for his children to attend a better school because he got a promotion at work after listening to the tips in your online course, it will help you to always remember what's truly important.

My Age is an Issue

I've heard people say, "I'm not old enough".

There are a set of people who will pay for your online course because you are young. They believe that you will come with a fresh twist.

If, on the flip side, you are also saying, "I'm too old", there are a set of people who will pay for your online course because you are old. They believe that you will come with a certain wealth of experience.

I want you to see what I'm saying.

The world is now a global village, and there will always be a set of people all across the world, who like you the way you are.

Please stop listening to those voices telling you that you are not good enough. They are lying to you.

Find Your Unique Factor

If, indeed, you are not good enough to teach a particular online course, there are other topics that you are probably very qualified to teach. Your job is to find that topic and to find a set of people who are willing to pay you to teach it.

In some cases, you might feel as if you are not good enough because you are comparing yourself to someone else who appears to be better than you.

Let's establish this fact first. Everyone else is different from you.

They might be better than you in a particular area, but there are also other areas where you have the upper hand.

Look out for the things that are different about you and start highlighting them.

Have you achieved something that the other person has not achieved? Have you experienced something that the other person has not experienced?

Your customers will choose you because of what is different about you. 'They will choose you because of that experience you have gone through. They will feel that they can connect with you better, especially if they are going through the same thing.

Please breathe easy.

You are enough.

There are people out there waiting for it and they will buy your online course because they like you just the way you are.

I Want it to Be Perfect

I've also heard people say, "What if my work is not good enough? What if nobody likes it?"

When you create something, it's deeply personal because it's your thoughts and ideas that you are putting forward, and it's hard to accept the criticism that will come with it.

You might be saying things like:

"I need my course to be perfect..."

"I won't launch my course until I can get this tiny thing right..."

Let me quickly put you out of this misery. There is no such thing as a perfect course, as there will always be room for improvement. This is the beauty of the creation process. Launch the first version, get corrections, and then launch it again.

When you hide your gift because you are scared that nobody will like it, the truth is you are probably focusing more on yourself than on the people who actually need your help.

A part of our brain will always wonder about what people will say, whether they will like it, whether anyone would buy it or whether our course is good enough. This thought comes so as to help you to give your best, but your best will never be enough.

If you look at your online course some years later, you will see areas that can be improved, and you will keep improving, so just start.

The desire to produce an online course that everyone will approve of can be a very dangerous path to follow because it will stop you from putting your work out there for others to see.

You will find yourself coming up with all sorts of excuses on why you can't launch your course, and you'll end up not launching at all.

There will always be people who will criticize everything you do and will never pay for your online course. It's okay.

You can't please everybody.

You were not sent to them.

Never lose sight of the people you whose lives will be impacted by your course; they are your real audience and they will thank you for creating your course.

Reflections

Moses also felt like he was not good enough.

He pleaded with the Lord,

"O Lord, I'm not very good with words. I never have been, and I'm not now, even though you have spoken to me. I get tongue-tied, and my words get tangled."
– Exodus 4:10 (NLT)

I can only imagine God's frustration at Moses.

Then the Lord asked Moses,

"Who makes a person's mouth? Who decides whether people speak or do not speak, hear or do not hear, see or do not see? Is it not I, the Lord?
Now go! I will be with you as you speak, and I will instruct you in what to say."
– Exodus 4:11-12 (NLT)

But Moses again pleaded,

"Lord, please! Send anyone else." **– Exodus 4:13 (NLT)**

Then the Lord became angry with Moses.

This is how you are also upsetting the Lord.

He's telling you to go and save His people, and you are telling Him about your mouth, your face, your ears or your nose?

Really? Are you going to keep saying that to God? The one who designed you carefully and wonderfully?

I DON'T WANT TO MAKE A LOT OF MONEY

When I was in secondary school, one of my classmates always used to say:

"Let me die before I become rich. I don't want to become rich and miss God".

That classmate of mine is dead today.

The fear of success is real, and I've seen it hold so many people back from doing anything to make an extra stream of income, such as launching their online courses.

My classmate held on to the belief that if she became rich, she would not be able to please God and that it was better for her to die first.

Her case might seem extreme but let me point out some more scenarios for you.

- *If I make a lot of money, I'm afraid that I might not be a submissive wife.*

- *If I become rich, I'm afraid that I will lose my friends. I don't want to become like Cynthia, she completely changed when she started making money.*

- *If I launch my online course and become successful, I'm afraid that I will lose my privacy and attract stalkers into my life. I don't think I will be able to handle all the scrutiny and criticism on social media.*

- *What if many people buy my online course, and I can't deliver on what I promised?*

Our fears are so irrational.

They are trying to protect us from seeming danger but they can also stop us from achieving bigger things.

The first step to overcoming your fear of success is to acknowledge it.

You can't solve a problem if don't agree that you have a problem.

Acknowledge the fears that you have, and then address them.

One way to address the fear of success is to remember that you have the power to choose.

You can decide what type of successful person you want to be.
You can decide to be financially successful and still be a submissive wife.
You can decide to be financially successful person and still be very nice to your friends.
You can decide to be financially successful and still love God.
You can decide to control what people learn about you on social media.

If you are afraid that you might launch your online course and not deliver on what you promised, instead of spending time worrying, spend that time instead, thinking of what you can do to deliver on what you promised.

Being successful is not a bad thing.

Success helps you to impact the lives of people, and you can decide to be the type of successful person who uses their wealth as a force for good in the earth.

Not all successful people are thieves. Not all successful people are corrupt. Not all successful people are wicked.

The fact that you know some successful people who stole or engaged in shady practices to become successful does not mean that you will steal or become corrupt because you want to be successful.

We need to make a decision to allow ourselves become successful so that we can be better role models and show people other ways success can look like.

We need more role models.

Please don't allow the fear of success stop you.

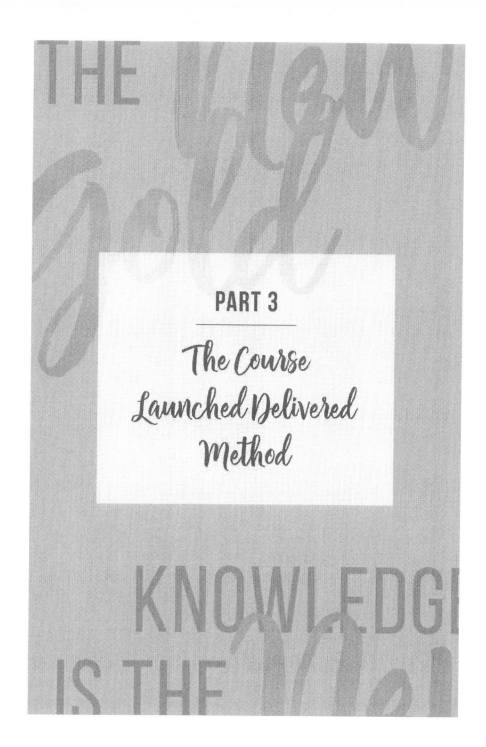

PART 3

The Course Launched Delivered Method

Back in 2014, I was so excited at the opportunity to earn income through online courses. I had created my first online course and I was amazed at the result.

At some point, the money I was earning from my Ankara accessories online course, was the same amount of money I was earning from my 9 - 5, where I was spending all my time doing work that I really was not passionate about.

Online courses looked like my way out...and boy oh boy!!! I took the risk.

I kept saying to myself, "If I can earn this amount of money from one online course that I created and now runs on autopilot, how much money will I make if I create more online courses?"

I resigned my job and started 2014 with so much excitement.

I was going to make so much money. I was going to BLOW!!! Hahaha! I'm sure you can guess what happened to me in 2014. Blowing was the last thing I did.

In fact, I did a lot of CRYING...

...because I launched online course after online course and can you guess how much I made from these new online courses?

$54.

What I did not realise is that, there were several things I did to make my first online course profitable. If I did not repeat those same things for my other online courses, I would not make any money from them.

I retraced my steps and worked on creating a system of launching profitable online courses.

This is what I now call **"The Course Launched Delivered Method".**

The Course Launched Delivered method is my signature process of creating, launching and delivering online courses that will make you money and impact lives.

To launch an online course that attracts students who will pay for your course, scream your name from the rooftops and pray for you consistently for changing their lives, there are 5 major steps you need to take:

1. Pick your course topic
2. Structure your online course
3. Grow your course audience
4. Plan your course launch
5. Create your course content

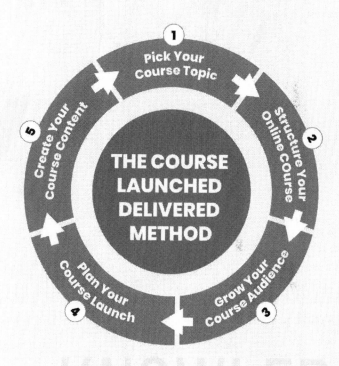

In this section of the book, I'm going to run you through all these steps.

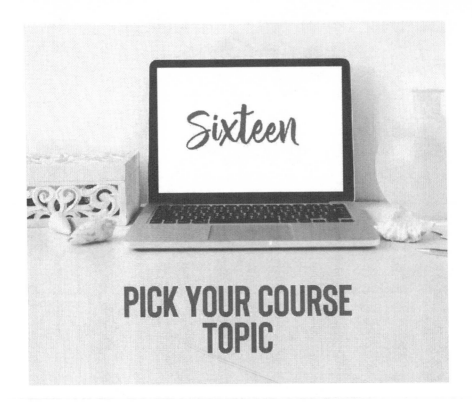

PICK YOUR COURSE TOPIC

There are three major issues people face when picking an online course. They typically say:

1. I don't know what to create an online course on
2. I have so many ideas, I don't know which one to pick
3. I'm not sure if my idea is profitable

Let's address these challenges one after the other.

I don't know what to create an online course on

The reason why this happens is that we take what we know for granted. Sometimes it's right under our noses, but we don't consider it as a valuable skill because it has always come to us easily. We don't realise that not everybody is having it that easy.

For example, I always thought that using web applications was easy. Just click here, click there and then click here. Until I started meeting people who were terrified of anything technology and already branded themselves as "I'm not a tech person".

Some people tell me, "I studied Biochemistry in school. I'm not sure I can teach Biochemistry, who wants to learn that?" First things first, realise that the course you studied in school is not the only subject you know. Life itself is a teacher. There are so many experiences that we have passed through that have taught us deep lessons about life and business. The question is, were you paying attention?

I like to call these experiences "teachable moments", because they teach us tangible lessons.

These moments come in three forms.

1.   Painful experiences
2.   Praise experiences
3.   Process experiences

Painful Experiences

Often times, we learn profound lessons when we go through painful experiences. For example, when I organised my first workshop and nobody paid for it, it was a very painful experience, but that was the beginning of a new learning experience.

I realised that the way I was marketing was not effective enough and I started learning other marketing strategies which helped me to sell out my workshops in the coming years.

Today, I can teach about how to market a workshop because I went through that painful experience and came out of it with lessons learnt.

Praise Experiences

This happens when we experience something that people praise us about. For instance, when you hit your target at your place of work or you deliver a presentation that causes people to give you a standing ovation.

You have achieved something significant and chances are...there's so much you know about achieving that result. It didn't just happen. If everybody could do it, it wouldn't have been such a big deal.

If you pay attention, you will notice that people will keep coming to you to ask, "How did you do it?" or "Come and teach me how to do xyz like you".

Our usual response is just to laugh it off, but there's a gold mine there. If one person is asking you how you did it, then there are a thousand more people also wondering… "how did she do it?"

Process Experiences

Any experience where you had to learn a process to achieve results, is a process experience.

For example, building a website, making accessories, organizing events, and so on are all process experiences. Nobody came into this world knowing how to build a website or how to make accessories. We all had to learn. When we were learning these skills, there were steps we had to follow to achieve results. If you have mastered the steps, you can easily show people how to follow the steps too.

Let me tell you why people pay to learn about a process. Not everybody has the time to figure out how to use or do something well. They are probably spending over 10,000 hours learning a different skill and don't want to spend another 10,000 hours learning this new skill too.

They just want someone who has figured out how to do it, to show them how they did it and this is where you come in.

What do you know how to do?

I have seen online courses on Microsoft Excel, cooking, programming, tennis, dancing, etc.

Don't despise what you know.

The best way to get all your teachable experiences out of your head is to brainstorm.
In Chapter 3, we shared a brainstorming exercise to help you to think of topics you can possibly teach.

If you didn't do that exercise, please go back there to complete it.

If you did that exercise properly, you should be faced with a different problem:

I have too many course ideas, I don't know which one to pick

This is actually a good problem, because it means that you ha

The best way to make a decision is to come up with criteria th
to eliminate some course ideas.

All course ideas are not equal.

If you run your course ideas through the criteria, you will discover the course that you are best suited to teach.

I use the phrase "best suited" because the fact that you know something does not mean that you should create an online course on it, especially if you want to make money. There are many other factors that you'll have to consider when you are deciding on what course to create.

Here are 5 Questions to Ask Yourself About Your Course Idea.

1. **Is there already a market of people who want to pay to learn this topic?**
No matter how passionate or knowledgeable you are about this topic, if there is nobody who wants to learn this topic, nobody will pay for it.

I know that this may be heartbreaking, but you know what is more heartbreaking? Doing all the work of creating an online course and then realise that nobody wants it.

This makes me remember one of my exploits a few years ago. I got inspired to make Ankara polo t-shirts. I was so excited about the idea and I thought it was super creative. I shared the idea with my friends, and they also thought it was creative. I could not believe that no one else had thought about the idea.

I set out to create my own line of African-inspired t-shirts. I spent countless hours doing research on how to make t-shirts. I researched on what fabrics to use, what machines were needed, where to source materials, where to find tailors, etc.

I bought machines, set up a factory, hired tailors, bought fabrics and produced my first collection. I imagined that I would run out of the t-shirts quickly and so I produced 100 pieces.

I had no doubt in my mind that I would sell out within a few weeks.

It took me two years to sell out those t-shirts.

In fact, I clearly remember the person that bought the last one.

I heaved a sigh of relief...finally!

I struggled to sell those t-shirts because I never paused and asked myself...are there people who are looking for Ankara polos to buy?

If they are, where are they? Can I reach them?

The same is true for online courses, and to be honest, any other business endeavour.

Sometimes, the market is not ready for what you want to teach and you may need to spend some more time educating the market about the importance of your topic before they will see the need to pay more to learn about it.

To know if there is a market for your topic, here are few signs you will notice:

1. Different people will keep asking you questions about the topic. They will invite you for private meetings because they want to pick your brain? They will send you private messages asking for help.
2. Other people may have written books, recorded YouTube videos, or even launched online courses concerning the topic.
3. You will find some people who are willing to pay for the course, even before you create it.

2. **Are you ready to teach this topic?**
   It's one thing to know about a topic, but it's another thing entirely to be able to teach a topic.

   To teach a topic, you must have gotten tangible results with undeniable proof. It helps if you even have testimonials from other people who can attest to how good you are.

   It has to be a topic that you are really comfortable with because your students are going to ask you all sorts of questions, and will be grossly disappointed if you can't give them sufficient answers.

When I was in primary school, my teacher always used to say, "If someone wakes you up from sleep and asks you this question, you should be able to answer it immediately".

I say the same thing too about the topic you want to teach.

If you are a bit honest with yourself, you will know whether you can teach this topic.

I've heard stories about people who go online, copy other people's work and pass it off as their own. This is actually a crime punishable by law.

It does not even make sense. If you have to copy someone else's work because you want to teach an online course, then it just means that you are not supposed to be teaching that topic. There would be some other topic that you are exceptionally good at.

Why choose to be a copycat when you can be the best in your own space?

3. Is this a topic you want to be known for?

When you launch a course, a lot of people will know you for the course that you launched, so in a lot of ways, your course will be a powerful branding statement.

There is also the launch phase where you will have to market your course. It's going to be very difficult marketing a course when you don't really want people to know that you are the one who created it.

Before people pay for the course, they look at the profile of the person who created the course and they make a decision about whether you are credible enough to teach them before paying for the course.

It's not really possible to create a course and hide your identity, because people buy courses from people.

I once spoke to a lady who told me, "All my friends come to me for relationship advice, but the truth is, I'm not comfortable branding myself as a dating expert."

This is absolutely fine.

Man, know thyself.

4. Is this something you are willing to pay to learn?

If you were to go back in time to a period when you did not know anything about this topic, if someone presented you with an online course on this topic, would you have paid for it?

If you find advanced classes on this topic, will you pay to improve yourself?

This question is important because your course idea has to make common sense to you. If you secretly do not believe that anybody will pay for your course, you will find yourself sabotaging all your plans.

You will eventually give up after convincing yourself that nobody would pay for it.

You'll probably not see the potential until you see another person launching a course on that topic and showcasing testimonials from their students.

5. Is there anything unique about the way you have gotten results in your topic?

This is particularly useful when you are teaching a topic that other people have already taught.

It might appear intimidating and you might be asking yourself,

"Who am I to teach this topic when this other person has taught this topic?"

The mistake a lot of people make is to copy what their predecessor has done and to offer it at a cheaper price.

This is a mistake because you might be short-changing yourself.

Low prices are often an indicator of low quality and there are people who are looking for high quality. There are also other factors apart from price that people consider when they are about to make a buying decision.

If you find yourself in this situation, what you can do instead is to ask yourself this question

"Have I gotten results in a different way from this person?"
"How am I different from them? "
When you find what is different, highlight your difference.

People will come to you because of that difference you are highlighting and you will easily stand out in the marketplace.

As you ask yourself these questions, you will find that there are topics that you are ready to teach and others that you are not ready to teach. You will also discover if there is a ready market for the topics you have in mind.

All course ideas fall under one of the following categories:

Cash Cow:
A cash cow is a topic you are ready to teach which people are willing to pay for. In fact, you can even generate a waiting list of people who want to pay for your online course before you create it.

For example, my course "Creating and Selling Online Courses" was a cash cow for me because I was ready to teach it. I had so much experience and results to show with regards to creating online courses and I also had a list of people who wanted to learn how I was launching online courses.

THE COURSE IDEA MATRIX

	READY TO TEACH	
NO MARKET	FARM LAND	CASH COW
	NO GO AREA	FUTURE LAND
	NOT READY TO TEACH	READY MARKET

Farm Land:
A farmland is a topic you are ready to teach but people are not really interested in paying to learn. They might not even know why that topic is important. I call it a farm land because you probably have to do a lot of education to alert people about its importance before they can get interested in learning more or even being willing to pay to learn.

No Go Area:
As the name implies, a no-go area is a topic you have no business in. You are not ready to teach it and there is no demand for it.

Future Land:
A future land is a topic that you are probably not ready to teach because you are still figuring things out. In a few years' time, you would have demonstrated impressive results in the topic and you can then teach others based on your experience.

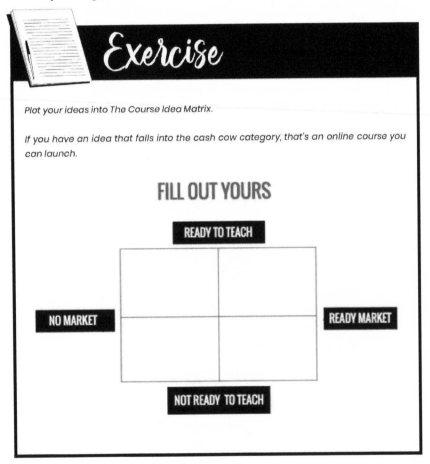

Plot your ideas into The Course Idea Matrix.

If you have an idea that falls into the cash cow category, that's an online course you can launch.

FILL OUT YOURS

READY TO TEACH

NO MARKET

READY MARKET

NOT READY TO TEACH

I'm not sure if my course idea is profitable.

In the Course Launched Delivered online course, we spend a lot of time validating your online course idea because this is a very valid concern.
You can never tell if your online course idea will be profitable until someone actually pays you.

Some people can tell you in a survey that they will pay for your course, but when you create the course, you may not see their brake lights again.

The only way to know whether people will pay for your course is when they actually pay for your course.

If you can get them to pay for your course even before you create it, that will be the icing on the cake.

This is actually a strategy called pre-selling and it's been used in other industries too.

Have you ever given someone selling a product a deposit, before receiving your product? That's the same way it works.

If you pre-sell your course and nobody pays for it...it's a bitter pill to swallow but at least you know, that it was not a profitable idea anyway and there's no point creating the course.

There are times I have pre-sold an online course and nobody paid for it. I just went back to the drawing board and restructured the course. I launched it again and this time around, I earned an income from it.

If people don't pay for your online course, it's just feedback.
There's something wrong somewhere and you can fix it.

Before we leave this chapter, I want to address this concern raised by a set of people.

"Do I have to choose a topic? Can't I do everything?"

If you chase two rats at the same time, you might catch none.

You can launch multiple courses, but you can't launch them at the same time.

You have to launch them one after the other, and at every point in time, you always have to decide, "What is my priority at this moment?"

I must also add that launching many courses on different topics might also affect your brand.

People might perceive you as a "Jack of all trades and master of none" and would prefer to go to a specialist who focuses on one topic.

You can pick one online course that you want to be known for and keep relaunching that course annually or multiple times a year. That course will become your signature online course because that's what people will know you for.

You will also get better at teaching that topic.

For the multi-passionate at heart, who really want to do so many things, I often advise that you can teach some topics for fun and for the fulfilment it gives you, but don't teach every course idea you are passionate about for a fee. People will end up not even knowing what to come to you for.

Exercise

Write out the outline of your online course.

_____

_____

_____

_____

_____

Write out the modules and the lessons that will go under each module.

_____

_____

_____

_____

_____

STRUCTURE YOUR COURSE TOPIC

The structure of your course refers to the way your course content is arranged and presented to your students. If your course is properly structured, it determines whether you will:

- Actually impact lives
- Get solid testimonials from your students
- Get referrals
- Get an opportunity to keep increasing the price of your course
- Get increased testimonials

Your course structure is made up of:

1. The outline
2. The content
3. The delivery
4. The support

The Outline

Before you set out to start creating content, you have to first of all, sit down and ask yourself the following questions:

"Who am I creating this online course for?"
I know you probably want to help a lot of people, which is why you are considering online courses in the first place, but you can't help everybody with a single online course because one person's problem is usually different from another person's problem.

Yet, there are a group of people who have the same type of problem and they can all take your online course. However, you have to be clear about the exact type of person who needs your online course. What problems are they going through?

When you understand the problem they are experiencing, it's easier to know what content to include in your online course.

Remember, your online course is not just packaged information. It is a training program that has been designed to solve a very specific problem that a particular set of people are experiencing.

"What is the result I want my ideal client to have after taking my online course?"
It has to be a tangible result that anybody can see.

Remember, you are taking your students on a journey and they have to be clear on when they have arrived at their destination.

You also have to be clear on where you are leading people to, so that you can guide them to that place through your online course.

"What is the transformation they have to go on to help them achieve that result?"
Ask yourself:

What is the first thing they have to do to achieve that result?
What is the second thing they have to do to achieve that result?
What is the third?

Keep going.

When you get to the end, you have the first draft of your course outline.

YOUR ONLINE COURSE

PROBLEM   TRANSFORMATION   RESULT

(YOUR ONLINE COURSE)

Designing an outline also helps you to save time when it's time to actually create the content because you know exactly what to include in every lesson.

Modules and Lessons

The outline of an online course is usually broken down into modules and lessons.

A module is a subtopic of your course.

Ideally, every major step you listed as you were drafting your outline should be classified as a module.

To achieve every step (or module), your ideal client probably needs to know and understand certain things; these are what you will then create as the lessons.

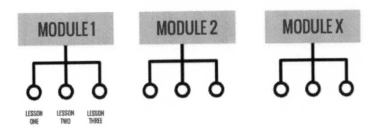

A lesson is a distinct point that will help your ideal client to achieve the outcome of a particular module. To come up with lessons, brainstorm on every question your ideal client is having that is stopping her from achieving the goal of the module.

To make this practical for you, I have written down the outline of my signature online course, Course Launch Delivered which helps people to create, launch and deliver their online course in 90 days.

You will notice the modules and the lessons under it.

Here is the outline:

A. **Pick Your Course Topic:** By the end of this module, you should have selected your course topic.

  1. *Brainstorm:* How to uncover the valuable expertise you can't see that is right under your nose
  2. *Eliminate:* How to decide which of your ideas is worth your time and energy so that you don't waste months chasing shadows
  3. *Validate:* My proven method to test whether people will pay for your online course even before you create it. You cannot kill yourself for nothing!

B. **Structure Your Course Content:** By the end of this module, you should have designed your course outline.

  1. *Ideal Client:* The number one thing to start with when structuring your online course is to get people to realise that you are the main deal
  2. *The Outline:* What to include in your course content if you want it to actually impact lives. If you do this right, you are going to get more than enough testimonials; you won't even know what to do with them.
  3. *The Title:* How to select a title that will make people say, "I have to have this course, what's your account number?" Getting this wrong can cost you 5 figures.
  4. *Pricing:* How to price your course perfectly, so that you don't waste a lot of time thinking about this.

C. Grow Your Course Audience: By the end of this module, you should have set up the tools you need to grow an audience who will pay for your online course.

1. *Goals:* How to strategically prepare for your launch by starting with the end in mind.
2. *List Building:* How to easily set up the four tools you need to attract the people who will pay for your course and how to prepare them for what's coming.
3. *Pages:* How to easily set up the three pages you need to grow your course audience.
4. *Simple Tech Training:* Step-by-step tutorials on different email service providers.

D. Plan your Course Launch: By the end of this module, you should have planned out your marketing strategy to sell your online course.

1. *Launch Plan:* How to strategically plan your launch so that you know what to do on Day 1, Day 2, Day 3...down to Day 60
2. *List Building Strategies:* How to drive the right set of people to join the waiting list of your online course so that you don't launch your course and hear crickets.
3. *Pre-Launch Content:* The exact content to create before your launch that will prepare your prospective students to buy your course.
4. *Social Media Posts:* How to create hype around your online course on social media.
5. *Launch Emails:* The specific emails you need to send to turn people from subscribers to buyers.
6. *Sales Pages:* How to write a highly compelling sales page that gets people to pay for your online course, even without meeting you in person.
7. *Urgency:* How to use urgency to get people to buy your course now, not later, without sounding scammy.
8. *Course Graphics:* How to design your course images, so that people can visualize what they are buying *(Hint: People don't buy what they don't understand)*

E. Create your Course Content: By the end of this module, you should have created your lessons and uploaded them on your online school.

1. *Lessons:* What to include in your lessons, so that your students can easily understand, even if you have never taught before.

2. *Video Production:* How to easily produce video lessons on a budget.
3. *Set up Online School:* How to set up a platform to host your course content so that the people who did not pay for it do not access it.
4. *Design Learner Experience:* How to give your students a pleasurable experience while they are in your online course, so that they scream how amazing your course is from the rooftops.

The Content

When creating content, the most important thing to consider is the learning style of your ideal client.

Everybody learns differently.

Some people are visual learners, which means that they learn better when they see pictures, images, diagrams, colours and so on.

Some people are aural learners, which means that they learn better when they hear sounds, rhythms, recordings, music and so on.

Some people are verbal learners, which means that they learn better when words are used. They prefer to read the words and even to read them aloud.

Exercise

Write out the outline of your online course.

Write out the modules and the lessons that will go under each module.

Some people are physical learners, which means that they learn by doing. They learn when they use their bodies in the process of learning, for example, by drawing diagrams or participating in live demonstrations.

Bearing this in mind, there are three major types of course content you can create:

1. Video
2. Audio
3. Text

I recommend video courses because videos appeal to visual learners, aural learners and even verbal learners if you add some text to the videos. You can also appeal to the physical learners by showing them what you want them to do, via video.

Another great thing about video is that you can repurpose your video content.

For example, if you record video lessons, you can pull out the audio recording and offer it as an option to people who prefer audio.
Another way you can repurpose video content is by transcribing them and offering this as an option to people who prefer text.

Every lesson should also have assignments, to help people implement what you have just taught them, otherwise it will go into the reservoir of things they have learnt but never used.

Free Content versus Paid Content

A question I get all the time is, "what should I include in my course? What should I give out for free and what should I give out for a fee?"

This simple diagram below explains this concept.

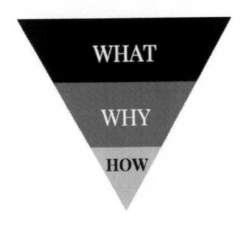

With your free content, you teach "The What" and "The Why".

With your paid content (in this case, your online course), you teach "The How".

For instance, if your course is about Intentional Parenting, in your free content, you can talk about what intentional parenting means and why it's important. You can even share a high level summary of how to go about it, but when it comes to the nitty-gritty of intentional parenting, this is what you want to include in your online course.

The people who want to know "The How" will pay for your online course.

I've seen people who share "The How" with others on Social Media and get frustrated when people don't apply what they shared.

People value what they pay for.

If you keep sharing "the how-tos" so freely, a lot of people might not even recognise the gems you are giving to them.

Delivery

The delivery refers to how you arrange your course content and make it easily accessible for the people taking your course. It also considers how you protect your course content so that people who have not paid for it cannot have access to it.

There are several options you can consider to host your online course, and I dare say that there is an option for everyone.

You can use:

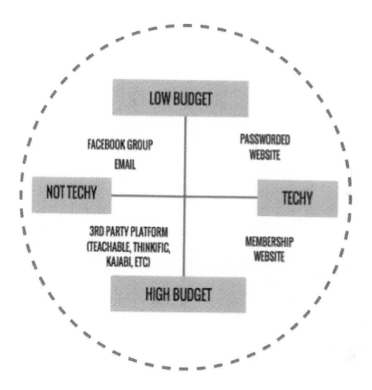

Passworded Pages

This is a password protected webpage on your website that restricts people from accessing your content, except they have the password.

It's easy to set up if you have a website, and it's also an option you can use if you are on a budget and you don't want to spend any money at all.

The downside is that the passworded page has only one password and this password can easily be sent to people who did not pay for the course.

If you are very particular about protecting access to the contents of your online course, I will not advise that you use this delivery method.

Membership Websites

A membership website is a protected website that only allows people who have been granted access to content that has been protected.

It generates individual usernames and passwords so that you can give those to the people who have paid for the course.

Most membership websites also have a way of tracking when different people are using the same username and password to sign in to the course.

It is the most secure way of delivering an online course.

It's also a great option to use when you have a lot of lessons to teach and you want them to be neatly organised.

For instance, my signature online course, Course Launched Delivered has a lot of lessons.

In my membership website, I neatly arrange all the lessons under each module and the participants can access all the lessons by visiting the module page.

It can be capital intensive at first, but in the long run, it's a cost effective option because you can use one membership website to host multiple online courses and you don't have to pay a monthly recurring fee to keep your courses on the website.

Another major advantage of using a membership website is that you can customise it to suit your brand aesthetic. If you are very particular about giving your clients a high class experience, which encourages trust and displays professionalism, this is the option to go for.

The downside is that it requires a good deal of time and technical competence to set it up.

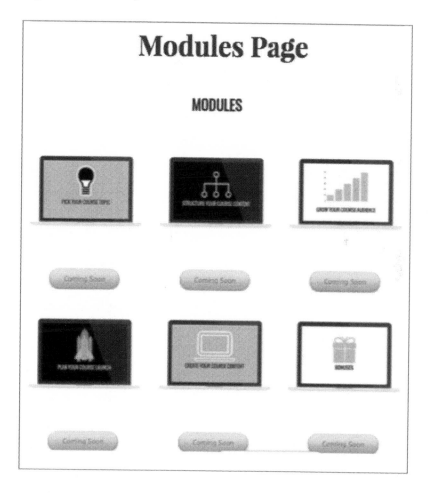

My team and I have however solved this problem by creating pre-designed membership websites.

This means that you don't have to set it all up by yourself. You can just buy a membership website that has already been set up for you and also has all the other pages you need to create and launch your online course.

To find out more about this, visit www.stephanieobi.com/coursewebsite

3rd Party Websites
3rd party websites were introduced because a lot of people were trying to launch online courses but got scared because of the technical requirements of building an online school to host their content.

Third party websites allow you to set up an online school with just a few clicks.
They have made it very easy for anyone to have an online school.
The draw back is that you have to pay a recurring monthly fee or a commission to use them. In the long run, you might find that you are spending a lot of money to keep your online courses up on those platforms.

Popular examples include Teachable, Thinkific, etc.

Emails
If you don't have a budget for a website, you can just use a series of emails. This is only advisable for mini courses, where you don't have a lot of lessons.

If the course is a full blown transformational course, your students might just get confused and this will affect their overall user experience.

Closed Facebook Groups
A closed Facebook group allows you to restrict who can join your group. This means that you can invite people to your closed Facebook group and deliver the content to them.

To make it easy for your students to know where each lesson is, you can create a pinned post on your Facebook group that will outline all the lessons and the links to the content.

No matter what option you choose, the lessons must be clearly accessible and your students should know where to find each lesson.

Remember, one big reason people are paying for your course is because they want the lessons to be delivered to them sequentially in an organised manner.

If they end up being confused, the purpose of the online course has been defeated.

Support

There are two major types of courses, and they determine the type of support you should give to your clients.

With mini courses, you are helping your clients to achieve a particular step.

With transformational courses, you are helping your clients to achieve a series of steps that will help them get to their end goal.

As people take several steps for the first time, they will have questions and if they don't get answers to their questions, they are going to feel stuck.

This is why most transformational courses come with a support Facebook group or live Q and A sessions.

An example of a transformational online course is my signature online course, Course Launched Delivered.

As you may have seen with the outline, there are several steps that my clients have to take that appear daunting. To help them to resolve the challenges that come up, I created a closed Facebook group to answer all their questions and to give feedback.

From my experience, I have discovered that knowledge alone does not help people to get the results they need. Most people value feedback, accountability and encouragement when they are learning something new or doing something for the first time.

They also want to network with the other people who are taking the course with them. In my online course communities, many people have found new friends, and have even collaborated on business ventures together.

This is another strong reason why people pay for online courses.

The network.

As you structure your online course content, also design a support system for your students especially if you are launching a transformational online course.

Success Story

"I learnt how to test the market for the validity of my course idea, how to structure my course, price my course and deliver value."

Before coming on Course Launched Delivered, I struggled with procrastination and lacked knowledge on how to structure and price my course.

It was difficult creating time to actually launch a course based of my busy schedule running my online stores along with my one-on-one coaching services.

Course Launched Delivered helped me in so many ways.

I learnt how to test the market for the validity of my course idea, how to structure my course, price my course and deliver value.

The course also helped boost my confidence. I developed my website, built my email list and grew it to over 1,200 subscribers, and launched my course, The Online Store Framework which helps entrepreneurs to start, launch and grow profitable online stores.

The Facebook group community was very helpful, and filled with real people.

Stephanie, you are a gift to the world. I admire your tenacity, commitment and consistency.

Thank you so much.

Aderonke Abiona
eCommerce Entrepreneur and
Online Store Strategist
www.aderonkeabiona.com

GROW YOUR COURSE AUDIENCE

When you create a course, it's human beings that will pay for it, watch it and implement the lessons.

This means that you need to present the course to the people who need it.

The big question becomes, "How do I find the people who need it?"

This is why you need to grow the audience for your online course and this is where email list building comes in.

What is an Email List?

An email list is a collection of email addresses of people who have indicated interest in hearing from you. It consists of their names and email addresses.

When you build an email list of people who are interested in learning about your topic, you can easily present your course to them and make them an offer.

The more of your ideal clients who are on your email list, the more people you can sell your online course to.

Why Email Lists and not Social Media?

Social media is great, but it cannot substitute the place of an email list. Here's why:

1. **Email lists help you to attract your ideal clients**
   Anybody can follow you on social media but they may not necessarily be your ideal clients. The process of inviting people to join your email list weeds out the people who don't need your course. I will explain how later in this chapter.

2. **Emails help you to build trust**
   It's easier to build an intimate relationship via email. If you send an email to the people on your email list, it feels like a personalised message from you to them and they begin to feel like they have a relationship with you. If you consistently send these emails on a certain day and time, they begin to expect you in their emails, and with time, they will begin to trust that you will always be there. Once trust is established, sales becomes easy because people trust that if they send you their money, you will not run away with it.

3. **No restrictions with email**
   Social media restricts the number of people who can see your posts. If you have 1,000 followers, not all of those 1,000 followers will see your posts because of certain algorithms, so it's safer to have a way of communicating with your community with no restrictions.

Besides, social media platforms are owned by companies. If you build your followers on their platform and something happens to their platform, there goes your business. You won't be able to reach your audience anymore. It's better to be safe than sorry.

How to Get Email Addresses

You can easily get email addresses by giving out a gift that your ideal client really wants.
To get the gift, they will have to give you their names and email addresses so that you can deliver the free gift to their inboxes.

When you give them something valuable:

1. They will look out for your name in their inboxes, and this is where the relationship will begin. They will recognise you as someone who has something they need, and not a spammer who is sending them emails they are not interested in.
2. They will be impressed if your freebie was really good and will identify you as an expert. The mistake a lot of people make is to give really bad gifts because they're free. If you give out something of low quality, people will think that your entire business is low quality. Put your best foot forward.

Big Mistake

The big mistake I have seen a lot of people do is to buy email addresses or add people's email addresses to their email list without telling them.

This is just a waste of time because the people whose email addresses you have bought do not know you and will wonder why you are sending them emails.

They won't even want to have anything to do with you because they will consider you as a spammer who is trying to scam them.

List building is an ongoing journey and requires some level of effort, but it pays to do it the right way.

Email List Building Tools

Let's talk about the techy side of building your email list. Don't be scared, lol. You only need to set up these five things.
1. Freebie
2. Opt-in page
3. Thank you page
4. Autoresponder
5. Email service providers

Freebie

A freebie is the free gift that you give out to your ideal clients, to get their email address in exchange.

A good freebie should:

- Attract only your ideal client

- Solve a specific problem for your ideal client
- Create a desire to take your online course
- Be visually attractive

The freebie could be a:

- Checklist
- Workbook
- Email course
- Quiz
- Webinar
- Video training
- Audio training
- List of tools and resources
- Scripts
- Comparison table
- Guide
- Printable
- Planner
- E-book

Opt-in page

An opt-in page is the page where people can share their names and email addresses in exchange for your freebie.

A good opt-in page should:

1. Tell people what the freebie will help them do
2. Have clear call to actions, that tell people to sign up
3. Have social proof like testimonials or logos of places and platforms where you have been featured
4. Have an opt-in form that has name and email address entry fields.

Thank you page

A thank you page is the page sent to people immediately after they sign up for your freebie.

A good thank you page should:

1. Thank them for signing up

2. Give clear instructions on what they should do next. Example: Look for the freebie in your inbox

3. Ask them to share the opt-in page with their friends

Autoresponders

This is the email that delivers your freebie to the people who subscribed to your email list.

A good autoresponder should:

1. Be set up to be delivered automatically
2. Have your introduction, especially if they are meeting you for the first time
3. Contain the freebie
4. Give clear instructions on what the next steps are

Email service providers

Email service providers are platforms that allow you to manage your email lists.

- They receive the your email addresses from the opt-in pages automatically for you.
- They store the email addresses for you
- They send out your autoresponder for you
- They help you to send out emails to your subscribers
- They track the number of people reading your emails and other related statistics for you.
- Some of them even have opt-in pages and thank you pages that you can use.

Common examples are MailChimp, Aweber, ConvertKit, etc.

In the Course Launched Delivered online course, we offer step-by-step training on how to set up all these email list building tools.

Getting Your Freebie Out There

After you have set up all your list building tools, your next step is to get people to sign up for your freebie, so that the size of your email list can grow.

In the next chapter, I will share with you different strategies you can use to grow your email list.

Success Story

"I'm doing so many things I thought I could not do before. It's incredible what taking your courses has helped me to achieve and I know this is just the beginning."

I was worried about whether it was really possible to reach my goals because I have been trying to crack the internet for over 15 years now. Nothing I tried worked. My conclusion was that I sucked at marketing. This was my last try to make the internet work for me.

Stephanie helped me to resolve my struggles by working through my mindset issues, teaching me about growing an email list, building a website, writing sales pages and creating online products, etc.

I'm doing so many things I thought I could not do before. It's incredible what taking your courses has helped me to achieve and I know this is just the beginning.

My confidence has grown considerably. I also hit my income goal, and I have so many happy and thankful students who take my courses on how to use Montessori skills to create joyful, happy learning environments where children can thrive and succeed.

I have gotten lots of results from working with Stephanie. I was a bit apprehensive, as I am more reserved and she is always laughing, but she is passionate about her work. Her joy and laughter have lightened my days and made me less serious and more relaxed.

Ayopeju Falekulo
Founder, Addlo Montessori
Training Center
www.ayopejufalekulo.com

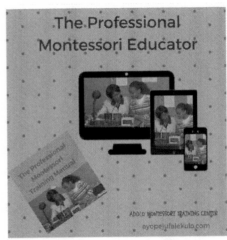

LIST BUILDING STRATEGIES

Email list building is the intentional process of growing an email list of people who are most likely to pay for your online course.

There are different strategies you can use to grow the size of your email list. You can:

1. **Send a message to your family and friends**
    You can write a compelling note to your family and friends and ask them to share with the people in their network. If you do this alone, you can get up to 100 new email subscribers

2. **Update your social media bios**
    All social media platforms have a section where you can describe yourself. You can use this section to tell people about your freebie and also include a link for them to sign up for it.

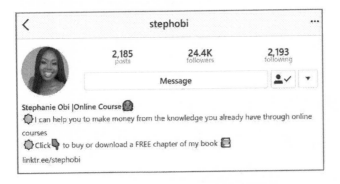

Visit all the social media platforms you have an account in, and update them. You may have accounts on Facebook, Twitter, Instagram, LinkedIn, etc.

PS: If you are not already following me on Instagram, now is a good time to search for me on Instagram and follow me. I share free tips all the time. My Instagram handle is @stephobi

3.   **Write great blog posts and set up your opt-in form on your blog**
Blog posts are very powerful because they help you to get found on Google.

Answer the frequently asked questions about your topic as several blog posts, and you will find that people who are looking for that content will find your blog especially if it is properly optimized for search engines.

[Case Study]: How to launch a Successful Flash Sale with Online Courses

Stephanie Obi | 3 Comments | June 28, 2017

I just rounded up my own flash sale of my online courses, and I was happy with the results.

In today's post, I decided to share with you my results, the steps I took to achieve it, and the mistakes I made so that you can avoid them.

When they get on your blog, there should be multiple places where they can opt in for your freebie.

You can have opt-in forms on your:
- Header
- Footer
- Sidebar
- Top menu bar
- In the middle of a blogpost
- At the bottom of a blogpost
- As a pop up
- About Me page
- Home page

Header

Sidebar

4. Ask the people who visit your blog to share your posts

If you want people to do this, you actually have to ask otherwise it might not cross their minds. If people share your posts with others, it will increase the number of people who see your posts and the number of people who get invited to sign up for your freebie.

You can also easily implement this by adding social media share links to the bottom of your blog posts.

5. Get featured on other people's podcasts or host your own

A podcast is really like having a radio show online. On your podcast, you can publish a series of audio recordings that people can listen to and download.

Podcasts usually have a lot of listeners from all over the world and you can get in front of new audiences by getting featured on other people's podcasts. If nobody has invited you to be featured on their podcast, you can pitch yourself to the owners of relevant shows.

They are always looking for interesting and inspiring content to share with their followers and if you have a great story around your brand, they will be happy to interview you.

You can also host your own podcast. There are platforms like iTunes and Stitcher which host podcasts. Anybody can visit these platforms to search for any topic, and they can find your podcast.

At the end of each podcast episode, you can invite people to sign up for your freebie.

6. **Get featured on a virtual summit or host your own**
A virtual summit is an online conference where different speakers gather to speak about a topic.

Each of the speakers in the summit are expected to share the details of the summit with their audience and this results in hundreds to thousands of people signing up to be a part of the summit.

It's a very attractive event because viewers can watch the sessions for free from the comfort of their homes.

When you present at a virtual summit, many people will be meeting you for the first time, and you can invite them to sign up for your super helpful freebie.

To get invited to virtual summits, you have to intentionally build relationships with other experts in your industry so that they can know what you do and invite you to speak at their events.

You can also host your own virtual summit and invite experts to be a part of it. I once hosted a virtual summit.

7. **Contribute to a popular blog that your ideal clients follow**

There are some blogs that receive guest articles from people. You can write to them, saying you would like to write about a topic their followers will like. Be sure to include what their audience will benefit from your article.

When you write the article that will be published on their blog, you can write about your freebie and include the link where they can get it from, or you can write about your freebie in the author's blurb.

An example of this is, "Stephanie Obi is an online business coach that helps people to create, launch and deliver online courses. She believes that everyone has some form of knowledge that they can share with the world and turn to profit. To sign up for her Online Course Starter Pack, visit www.stephanieobi.com/coursevip"

8. **Contribute in the Facebook groups that your ideal clients are in or host your own Facebook group**
Facebook groups are groups hosted on Facebook that bring together people interested in a particular topic.

These groups are typically led by someone who is the creator of the group, manages the affairs of the group and grows the community.

If they are doing a good job, the group members are usually engaged and genuinely want to learn more about the topic.

You can position yourself as an expert in the group by sharing relevant content in the group, so that people will be drawn to find out more about you and possibly sign up for your freebie.

Most Facebook groups have rules and regulations, so you can't just drop your freebie there and run, but there will be days when the host of the Facebook group will ask their members to promote their freebies, and you can share yours there.

You can also host your own Facebook group and share your freebie with everyone who joins your Facebook group. As at the time I wrote this book, Facebook advertises Facebook groups for free, so on any given day, you can have 10 to 100 new people requesting to join your Facebook group.

9. **Plan a viral giveaway**
A viral giveaway is slightly different from a giveaway.

A giveaway is a competition to win a prize, where every contestant only has one entry opportunity.

A viral giveaway is a competition to win a prize, where every contestant has multiple entries depending on whether they share the competition with their network.

To enter for the competition, they have to enter their email addresses.

If you make the prize of your giveaway specific to your online course, you can attract the people who really want to learn more about your topic.

For example, I once held a viral giveaway where the winner got a scholarship to Course Launched Delivered, my 90-day programme, which helps people to create, launch, and sell online courses.

Over 500 people entered for this giveaway and I was sure that these were people who were interested in launching online courses.

Viral giveaways also work because participants have to share the details of the giveaway to help them win. This increases the chances of more people seeing your giveaway and also signing up for it.

Even though everybody who enters the contest will not eventually win, you can give them your freebie and start building relationships with them.

Tools you can use to host your viral giveaway include Kingsumo, ViralSweep, etc.

10. Host a challenge on social media

A challenge is another great email list building strategy because it helps people to build trust in you quickly. The way it works is that you invite people to sign up for a challenge that helps them to achieve a very specific result.

Every single day of the challenge, you deliver a set of instructions to all the people who signed up, helping them to take action.
If people actually get results at the end of this challenge, their confidence level in you will shoot up and they will be more likely to pay for your online course because they trust that you can help them to get more results.

11. Run Facebook or Google ads

Adverts are a great way of promoting your freebie to people who are not within your circle of influence.

They are very effective because they show up on social media where a lot of people are spending time. If your advert is persuasive enough, they can easily sign up on the spot.

They also have advanced targeting features that help you to reach the exact people you want your advert to reach, irrespective of the country they live in.

They are also cost efficient compared to other different types of adverts because you can run an advert with any amount. You can also track whether they are working or not, and tweak the ads to improve their performance.

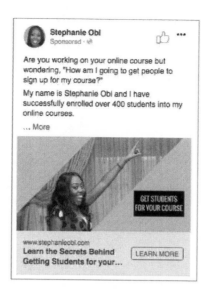

12. Sponsored posts on high traffic blogs

You can also promote your freebie on a blog that a lot of your ideal clients visit regularly.

I tried this once and I got over one thousand subscribers with just one post, and many of these people eventually paid for my online courses.

For your sponsored post to be effective, your post has to address a pain point your ideal client is having, and position your freebie as the solution to that problem. You must also ask people to sign up for your freebie. This is a call to action. If you don't ask people to perform an action, they may scroll away from that post and not do anything. It also helps for your image or video to be visually appealing.

13. Host a webinar

A webinar is a free live presentation, delivered online to viewers all over the world. It is particularly different from a Facebook Live or Instagram Live because people have to sign up to your email list to attend the webinar.

People who watch the webinar live can listen to you present and also ask you questions while you are still live. You can also share the replay with people who signed up for the webinar but could not make it live.

To reach an entirely new audience, you can host a joint webinar with someone else who will be presenting you to their audience as an expert.

Webinars are great for building trust because you will be giving your audience very valuable information for free and you can answer their questions on the spot.

14. **Get on TV or radio**

Even though it's not online, TV and radio platforms are still a great way of promoting your freebie.

An easy way to do this is to get interviewed.

At the end of every interview, the interviewer will typically ask what the best way to reach you is. You can then direct your viewers or listeners to your opt-in page.

I usually have an opt-in form on the homepage of my website, so that when I direct people to my website, the first thing they will see on the home page is an opt-in invitation to get my freebie.

15. **Go live on your platform or someone else's platform**

When you go live, the people who are following you on your social media page develop a stronger relationship with you because they get to see you live and hear you speak. You can use this opportunity to invite them to sign up for your freebie.

To reach an entirely new audience, you can also go live on some other person's platform, and at the end of your presentation, you can invite them to sign up for your freebie.

This is another reason why it is so important to build relationships with other people in your industry.

It's actually very easy to build relationships. You can simply start by helping other people. As you help them, you will be investing in their emotional bank account, so that when you eventually ask for help, the chances that they will say yes to you would be higher.

16. **Include your opt-in page on your business card and email signature**

This one is very simple to implement. You can include your opt-in page on your business card, so that when you go for events and you distribute your cards, the people who receive them can sign up for your email list.

You can also include the link to your opt-in page in all your email by adding it to your email signature.

17. **Say yes to speaking engagements**
Speaking engagements are a great way to grow your email list because when you speak, you are being presented to the audience as an expert.

As you speak, you can tell the audience about the additional resource you have for them on your website, which is your freebie, and you can tell them to sign up for it.

18. **Organise a live event**
You can also organise a free live event. This can be a simple networking event, a two hour workshop, book club meet-up, lunch and learn, etc. Look for a place that attracts your ideal clients and market your event. Encourage people to sign up and come with their friends.

At the event, you can have a registration stand, where people will put down their contact information including emails. Depending on the type of event you organised, you can share your freebie with them during your presentation and ask them to sign up for it, or you can then send them an email asking if they would like to sign up for your freebie, and share the sign up link with them in the email.

19. **Give testimonials**
This strategy is not so obvious, but it is an effective one. When you give testimonials to people whose products you have patronised, they put you in front of their audience by displaying your name and sometimes your website, on their own platform.

A lot of people are going to see that testimonial, and search for you. When they find your platform, they will see an invitation to sign up for your freebie, and will join your email list.

20. **YouTube**
Believe it or not, YouTube is the second largest search engine, as at the time of writing this book. You can start up a YouTube channel and start publishing video content on a regular basis. People will find your YouTube channel online when they search for keywords related to your videos.

You can also get featured on other people's YouTube channels. This will bring you in front of an audience that might have never heard of you.

In each of your YouTube videos, always encourage people to go to your website to sign up for your freebie. Please do not get carried away with amassing thousands of subscribers and forget to grow your email list. At the end of the day, YouTube belongs to a different organisation. They can wake up one day and change the rules. Your email list will always belong to you.

If you want to switch email service providers, you can carry your email list along. It is not tied to any platform.

The list of things you can do to grow your email list are inexhaustible. These are just some ideas to get your creative juice flowing. Please feel free to try out more ideas.

Due to the space limits in this book, we can't really go into the details of how to implement all these strategies, but we provide in-depth training on how to implement these strategies in the Course Launched Delivered online course

Leaving your Comfort Zone

A lot of these strategies will require you to leave your comfort zone. They will require you to become visible and this might feel uncomfortable if you are not used to putting yourself out there.
Becoming visible starts in the mind.

It starts by realising how amazing you are, even if no other person has said it to you before.

It starts from realising that other people need your help, and if you hide away, they will keep suffering.

It starts by accepting that not everybody will understand you, and that's okay. You've not been sent to everybody.

It starts by confronting the things you are really afraid of, and dealing with those fears.

It starts by deciding to remain consistent even though it feels like no one is watching or even responding.

It starts by realizing that your purpose is more important than what people say or how they feel.

It starts by deciding to do it anyway, even though your feet are shaking and you feel so scared.

One day, you will look back and say, "what was I even afraid of?"

I should have left that comfort zone, a long time ago.

Make a decision to feel the fear and do it anyway.

According to Jack Canfield, "Everything you ever want, is on the other side of fear".

Exercise

Which of these strategies will you use to grow your email list?

_____

_____

_____

_____

_____

_____

_____

_____

_____

_____

PLAN YOUR COURSE LAUNCH

As you build a community of people who are interested in learning about your topic, you also need to plan the launch of your course next.

According to Benjamin Franklin, "If you fail to plan, you are planning to fail".

The mistake a lot of people make is to create their course and hope that people will just sign up for it.

They argue that, "if you build the course, the customers will come".

This is the beginning of disappointments.
You have to create a buzz around your course, so that people will recognise your course as the solution to their problem and pay for it.

This is what launching your course entails.

What is a Launch?

A launch is a system of generating demand for your online course and getting people to pay for the course.

If you don't launch your course, people are just going to be sitting in your email list, and they won't even know that you have an online course available.

A launch helps you to:

- Sell your online course
- Become known as an expert in your topic
- Build a relationship with your online community
- Reach out to the people who really need your help

If this already sounds scary, look at it this way:

If you visited a good restaurant, would you recommend that restaurant to your friends?

I'm sure you would. You recommend good places, good books, good products and so on to your friends because you loved the experience there and you want them to also experience the same thing. That's the same way launching feels. You have an online course that can solve people's problems and you are recommending people to take it because you want to help them.

Do you like motivating people and getting them to take action?

I'm sure you do, and I guess you feel fulfilled when people actually take action because you know that they are on their way to having their problems solved. That's the exact way launching feels. If you have a great online course that will change people's lives, you also have to motivate them to take the course, so that they can get the results they are looking for.

Types of Launches

There are two major types of launches:

1. **Evergreen launch**
   This means that you will launch your course once and the course will be available for sale all year round.
   Pros:
   - People can pay for your online course anytime they discover you; they don't have to join a waiting list.

Cons:
- People might keep procrastinating and may never pay for your course.
- You have to keep marketing the course all year round.

2. **Open and close launch**

This means that your course will only be available for sale when the cart is open. Anytime you want to open the cart again, you will have to relaunch the course.

Pros:
- When you close the cart, your force people to make a decision, and you can make a lot of money during those few days
- Closed launches create a lot of buzz
- Students can go through the course together at the same time, which builds momentum and a sense of community
  - When you have a dedicated launch period, you can review your launch and improve on it
  - You can hire an assistant during your launch period
  - It helps you not to look like someone who is always trying to sell something. During the time your cart is closed, you can offer free content to your community to just build the relationship.

Cons:
- People who discover you when the cart is closed have to wait until you reopen it.

Launch Plan

A very common mistake course creators make is to send out a tweet or post an image on Instagram and say, "Hey guys, I've launched my online course", and then expect that sales will start rushing in.

To have a successful launch, you need to do so much more, and this is why it can feel overwhelming, because there are so many things that need to be done.

This is why you need a launch plan.

A launch plan outlines all the activities you need to do during your launch.

Creating a Launch Plan

1. **Set your launch goal**
   The first thing to start with when planning your launch is to decide on the goal of your launch.
   How much money do you want to make?
   This will determine the activities you need to do during your launch. The launch plan for a $270 goal is significantly different from the launch plan of a $27,000 goal.
   The higher your launch goal is, the more strategic you need to be, starting with the number of people that should be in your email list.

   According to industry statistics, 1 - 2% of the people on your email list will pay for your online course. This is often referred to as the conversion rate, because it measures how many people converted from email subscribers to buyers.

   $$Launch\ Goal = \frac{Number\ of}{Subscribers} \times \frac{Conversion}{rate} \times \frac{Price\ of\ your}{online\ course}$$

   The formula is:
   If you want to make more money, you can either increase the number of subscribers in your email list or increase the price of your online course.

   It is possible to increase your conversion rate by inspiring people to take action.

   If you find that money does not motivate you, you can also measure your success by the number of people you want to come on the online course.

   You can also calculate the number of lives who will be directly and indirectly impacted by your online course.

2. **Launch dates**
   When exactly do you want your launch to start?

   When do you want it to end?

If you don't set dates, you might discover that you just keep procrastinating over and over again.

I like to put all the dates that are important to my launch in a calendar that I look at everyday. It keeps me grounded.

You can also put the dates you will execute your plans in the calendar.

For example, if you want to publish a blog post as part of your launch, you can mark the date you will write your post in your launch calendar.

If you want an evergreen launch, this means that you will launch your course once and the course will be available for sale all year round.

If you want an open and close launch, it means that your course will only be available for sale when the cart is open. Anytime you want to open the cart again, you will have to relaunch the course.

3. **Brainstorm your free content**
Education is a crucial part of your launch, because it helps you to:

- Build a relationship with your community
- Build your credibility with your community
- Create a demand for your online course
- Help people to understand what your online course entails
- Help people to see what the benefits of taking your online course
- Give people a taste of what to expect if they come on your online course.
- Address topics that might be holding them back from taking your online course.

It's very important that you give value first, before asking people to pay for your online course.

When people join your email list, they are in different places.

Some people are aware of their problem, and already trust that you can solve their problems. When you present your course to them, they will pay for it without any delay.

Some people are aware of their problems but don't yet trust you. If you share free content with them, they can consume it and realise that you can help them. This might encourage them to pay for your online course.

Other people trust you, but are not yet aware that they have a problem. In your free content, you can tell stories that will make them realize that they have a problem that your online course can fix. Your free content will give them a wake up call.

Some set of people don't trust you and are not aware that they have a problem. They are not yet ready to take your online course and don't even need your free content. If they however continue to see you delivering free content, you will remain top of mind. The day they realise that they have a problem, they will reach out to you, consume your free content and pay for your course.

When you create your free content, create content for the different categories of people in mind.

Brainstorm on what your free content will be about.

It can be:
- Blogposts
- Videos
- Podcasts
- Webinars

- Livestreams
- Emails
- PDF guides
- Challenges

4. **Set up your sales page**

A sales page is a page on your website that outlines all the details of your course and how people can pay for it.

You need one because you cannot possibly speak to all the people who are interested in taking your course one-on-one.

It also helps you to communicate the value of your online course.

A good sales page should:
- Have a catchy headline
- Describe your online course
- Describe the benefits
- Describe your ideal client
- Have testimonials
- Have your bio
- Ask people to pay
- Have payment buttons or account details
- Answer frequently asked questions
- Be visually appealing
- Have a way people can contact you if they have more questions

5. **Set deadlines**

Deadlines are great because they help to add urgency to your course launch. If there is no urgency, people might keep procrastinating the decision to pay for your online course.

You can create urgency by:
- Offering discounts during your launch, e.g. early bird offers.
- Offering limited time bonuses during your launch, e.g. 48-hour bonuses.
- Offering a fast action bonus during your webinar or livestream
- Offering bonuses to a fixed number of people
- Closing the cart

You can also use countdown timers in your sales page and emails to let people know that a deadline is approaching.

6. Write launch emails

Emails are a must have during your launch. You can use them to educate, build excitement and urge people to pay for your course.

During your launch, you can send emails that:
- Share your story and why you created this online course
- Create excitement for your upcoming launch
- Inform your community about the different launch activities
- Explain what your course will entail
- Announce that your course is now open for enrolment
- Address objections
- Showcase testimonials
- Address frequently asked questions
- Announce deadlines
- Announce bonuses
- Say thank you

7. Create social media posts

As you send emails during your launch, you should also share posts on social media. This creates a synchronized hype and help you to remain top of mind among your ideal clients.

There are many different types of content you can post during your launch, but there are certain questions people ask themselves when they see you launch. You can use your social media posts to answer those questions.

Why should they learn from you?

Create a social media post, sharing your achievements, your story and why you are qualified to teach this topic.

When people are considering taking your course, they want to be sure that you are not just a scam.

Why are you interested in helping them?

There is a popular quote that says, people don't care how much you know until they know how much you care.

Create a social media post that shares how much you care about solving their problem specifically.

Why should they bother about this?

Create social media posts that describe the real benefits your online course will help they achieve and explain why they should want to have it. Show them how their lives will look like if they have these results

Why can't they do this later?
Create social media posts that explain why they need to act now, not later. Show them what will suffer if they procrastinate

Why should they work with you?
Create social media posts that show people why you are better positioned to help them than your competitors. Show they why your online course is a better solution to go with than any other substitute that might be in the market
As you create great content for your social media posts, back it up with great graphics. A great tool you can use to create eye catching graphics is Canva.

8. **Contact Affiliates**
This is optional, but if you decide to work with affiliates, this is also the time to contact them.

An affiliate is someone who markets your online course for you and gets a commission from every sale they bring.

You can give them a commission of 25 - 50% per sale.

9. **Decide on what to upsell and downsell**
Upselling is selling a product to people who paid for your online course. For example, one-on-one coaching, software, etc.

As you work with your clients, some people are going to need some extra support and you can create different packages for them.

Downselling is selling a product you sell to people who did not pay for your online course. For example, a cheaper online course, etc.

After you close your launch, there will be a set of people who could not afford your course, and you can offer them a cheaper online course.

Putting it all together

As you can see, there are quite a number of things you need to do to plan your launch. This is why I recommend that you create your own launch calendar.

To create one:

1. Write out everything you need to do.
2. Get a plain sheet of paper, and draw out 35 square boxes.
3. Plot dates and days into those square boxes.
4. Plot your to dos into specific dates.
5. Keep your calendar in a place where you'll see it everyday.

"I learnt how to test the market for the validity of my course idea, how to structure my course, price my course and deliver value."

Previously, when I launched an online course, I barely got up to 5 paying students.

After Course Launched Delivered, I launched one of my courses and I got close to 20 paying students.

It was a great success. I made 6 figures in naira.

My email subscriber list grew from 1000 to close to 4000 in just a short time.

Now my courses and landing pages are more professional, my conversion rates have improved a lot and I now know how to launch my online courses.

Rotimi Leigh
Cake Business Coach
www.bakingbusinessschool.com.ng

CREATE YOUR COURSE CONTENT

Your online course content comprises of the lessons, workbooks and resource guides.

Lessons

We actually started thinking through the lessons when we created the course outline. Your lessons are the things your students need to know and understand from your course.

A great lesson should include:

- **Definitions**
  Never assume that people understand what you are talking about. You may have gotten used to a term but it might be industry jargon to the people who are learning from you.

- **Why the topic is important**

If you don't tell people why a topic is important, they may not take it seriously.

- **Supporting materials**
  These are materials that support your topic like case studies, stories, quotes, statistics, research, etc.

- **Explanations**
  Come up with models, formulas, steps, etc. to explain your topic

- **Implementation**
  Come up with tools they can use to implement the topic. It's one thing to tell people what to do, but it's another thing to make it easy for people to do it.

  You can create workbooks, resource guides, how-to training, checklists, templates.

- **Your personality**
  Do things that are signature to your brand. For instance, I laugh a lot and in all my lessons, I intentionally launch and say things to make my clients laugh.
  You won't go very far if you try to copy others and do things that are not authentic. Your followers can tell.

Lesson structure

Lesson structure refers to how your lessons will flow from one step to the next.
When you design a structure for your lessons, it makes it easy to create the lessons.

Here's an example of a lesson structure
- Tell them what you are going to tell them
- Share a relevant story, quote, statistic
- Tell them what they need to know (the content)
- Ask them to take action (implementation)
- Tell them what you told them
- Tell them what's coming next

How many lessons should I create?

You can create as many lessons as it will take to help your clients get results. If you can make them succinct, that will be great because people are very busy.

The recommended length of your lessons should be 20 - 30 minutes.

Lesson format

You can create your lessons in:
- Video
- Audio
- Text

How can I create videos?

There are two types of videos you can create for your online course.

You can create a talking head video, where the camera is focused on you as you speak to it.

You can also create a screencast, which can record your computer screen. You can use screencasts if you are recording a lesson where you want to show people what is happening on your screen. This is very helpful for tech tutorials. You can show people what buttons you are clicking on, etc.

You can also use screencasts to record yourself speaking over your slides.

Talking head video

There are two straightforward approaches to creating this type of video.

You can either hire it out to a professional or you can record it yourself.

If you want to record your video yourself, you can use a DSLR camera or the webcam on your laptop or even your phone.
To use your webcam, you might need to invest in a webcam like Logitech c920 to improve the video quality.

To use your phone, you might need to mount it on a table tripod stand so that your phone can remain stable as you record.

Another factor that improves the quality of your video is lighting.

If you want to use sunlight, you can position your camera in front of a window, so that you are facing the window, which is the main source of light.

If you want to improve the quality of the video, you can also invest in some extra lighting.

You can start with a ring light or an umbrella lighting kit.

Screencasts

You can do a screencast of your screen where you show people what you are clicking on, on your screen. You can also do a screencast of your slides.

You can design your slides using Microsoft Powerpoint, Keynote for Mac or Canva.

There are different software you can invest in to record a screencast video. If you use Windows, you can use Screencast-O-Matic or Camtasia.

If you use a Mac, you can use Screencast-O-Matic or ScreenFlow.

Microphone

You can also use a microphone to improve the audio quality of your videos.

Popular options are the Blue Yeti and Audio Technica brand.

Editing videos

This might sound funny, but this is actually what I did when I started creating my own videos.

I didn't have time to learn how to edit videos and so I decided not to make any mistakes in my videos.

If I make a mistake, I would just say, "Sorry, I made a mistake" and move on.

If there was a serious problem with the video, for instance, an unexpected loud noise in the background, I would just record the video all over again.

If you are however not like me, and you don't mind learning how to edit videos yourself, you can use Windows Movie Maker if you work with Windows. Best part is, it's free.

If you use a Mac, you can use iMovie if you want a free option or Final Cut Pro or Adobe Premier Pro.

You can also just decide to outsource the editing.

Hosting videos

If you are hosting your courses on a website, it is not advisable to host your videos directly on your website, because videos files are quite large in size and can make your website so slow. Not to mention that people might not even be able to watch the videos.

Instead, you can use 3rd party platforms like Wistia or Vimeo to securely host your videos. They are different from YouTube because you can restrict the number of people who have access to your videos.

YouTube can be also used to host videos for your online course but YouTube is a social media platform that was designed to share videos. If you are keen on protecting your content, YouTube might not be the platform for this.

If you find that your video is too large, you can compress it to a smaller size before uploading it on a 3rd party website by using a tool like Handbrake.

How can I create audio lessons?

Like I explained earlier, you might want to give your clients an audio version of your lessons.

To create these audio lessons, you can simply record yourself speaking using your phone.

If you have already created a video and you want to use the same audio in your video, you can convert your video to mp3 using free online mp4 to mp3 converters.

How can I create workbooks and resource guides?

As you create your workbooks and resource guides, you need to be clear about the purpose of these guides and what you want your students to accomplish with each one you create.

The purpose of your workbook will guide the questions you ask people to answer in the workbook and will also guide on what to include in the resource guides.

The design tool

A simple tool you can use to create your workbooks and resource guides is Canva. It's a free tool and you can find it at www.canva.com.

Other options include:
- Adobe Acrobat DC
- Microsoft Word
- Microsoft PowerPoint
- Microsoft Publisher
- Apple Pages
- Apple Keynote
- Adobe InDesign

As you design your workbooks and resource guides, you can use design elements such as:
- Text
- Shapes
- Quotes
- Grids
- Pictures
- Graphics
- Tables
- Cover pages
- Copyright

When you are done, remember to save it as a .pdf file and to name it.

Finding time to create your course content

There's basically no right or wrong answer when it comes to creating time to create your course content.

Just create a schedule that works for you.

You can create a schedule based on the time you have available

I created my first online course while I was still engaged in a 9 - 5. To create my online course content, I had to take some days off work to record my video lessons, and then I used some weekends to work on the rest of the course.

You can create a schedule based on the number of lessons you have to create

When I was creating my signature course, Course Launched Delivered, I had so many lessons to create and I didn't wanted to get overwhelmed. I created the course content over a period of three months.

You can create a schedule based on how you want to deliver your course

There are two major ways of delivering your course content.

Your course can be self-paced.

This means that all your lessons will be delivered at once and your students can go through the lessons at their own pace. They can watch all the lessons in one day if they want to or slowly watch the lessons.

This means that all your lessons have to be available before you give your students access to the course.

Your course can be dripped.

This means that your lessons will be delivered one after the other, giving your students time to implement the lessons.

For example, you can give your students access to module one in the first week, and access to module two in the second week, etc.

This method helps your students to go through your course without feeling overwhelmed.

If you deliver your course this way, you only need to create 20% of your lessons before you admit students into the course.

As you give your students access to module one, you can be creating the content for module three.

This requires a high level of discipline. If you don't meet up with the lessons when you promised to deliver them, you might end up destroying your reputation.

Learning Experience

As much as you really want to share your content with your students, you also have to consider the learning experience.

The learning experience is how people feel when they are taking your online course. It determines whether people enjoy your course, complete it, recommend it, or even buy more of your courses.

The truth of the matter is that, whether you intentionally design an experience for them or not, your students are having an experience.

You can intentionally design a great one.

The most important question to ask is, "How do I want my students to feel as they are taking this course?"

This will inspire ideas on what you can do to give them a great experience.

One of the things you can do is to create your content with a great visual identity.
- Use colours that express how you want people to feel
- Use fonts that express how you want people to feel
- Find textures, patterns, etc. that you can use in your design
- Use high quality pictures

Another thing you can create are guides.

Your students might not know how to login to the school or what to do when they experience a challenge.

You can come up with:
- A starter pack
- Welcome emails
- Reminder emails

To make your clients fall head over in love with you, you can surprise them with things you did not advertise.

You can come up with:

• Live Q and A sessions: This is when you come on live to answer questions people might be having.
• Hot seats : This is when you take one person's situation and really dive into it in front of everyone else.
• One-on-one coaching: You can also decide to help people one-on-one.
• Accountability partners: You can set them up with accountability partners so that someone else apart from you can encourage them as they take the course.

At the end of the day, there will always be room for improvement.

Send your clients a message to give you feedback.

You can use positive feedback as testimonials, and you can use the negative feedback to improve your course. Negative feedback might be difficult to hear because when you are creating your lessons, you typically would pour out your heart. Don't take it personally. They might be bringing up things that you were not aware of. Just read through the lines and pick out the lessons.

At the end of the day, the quality of your course will be improved and it's still a win-win situation for you.

You can increase the price of your course and your new students will have a better experience.

What Next?

Now that you have been armed with the knowledge you need to create, launch and deliver your own online course, you might need some:

- Personalised feedback
- Mentorship
- Community of like minds also creating online courses
- Tech Support
- Accountability
- In-depth training

I provide all these through my products on www.stephanieobi.com

Course Launched Delivered Online Course

This is a 90-day online program where we work together to create, launch and deliver your online course.

In addition to the content and bonuses, we offer feedback on all your exercises, advice from my experience with online courses, tech training tutorials and support, and we also follow up with you in case you need some encouragement or a wake up call.

We only open this course for enrolment two times a year.

To sign up for the waiting list, kindly visit:
www.stephanieobi.com/courselaunch

Online Course Website

This is a membership website that has already been built for you. It includes all the pages you need to create and host your online course, and you won't have to pay any website designer or monthly recurring fees.
It comes with:

- Home Page
- Opt-in pages
- Thank you pages
- Sales page
- Webinar registration page
- Webinar thank you page
- Live webinar page

- Login page
- Courses page
- Module page
- Lessons page
- Shop page
- About Me page
- Sales page
- Contact page
- Free domain registration for a year
- Free website hosting for a year
- Social media integration

It also comes with 90-day support and will have your logo on it. All you will need to do is to customise the colours and fonts to your brand, and you can create as many more pages as you like.

To get your own online course website, kindly visit www.stephanieobi.com/coursewebsite

Speaking Engagements

If you need a speaker for your event, I'm open to delivering speaking engagements such as keynotes, expert panel discussions and workshops.

To find out more about my availability and list of speaking topics, kindly visit www.stephanieobi.com/speaking

Brand Partnerships

If you are planning a campaign or a programme that is tailored to your organization's specific needs, I'm open to collaborating with you on your unique campaign.
Our work together can include but is not limited to media campaigns, online videos, TV shows, live events, sponsorships, trainings, editorials, brand ambassadorship, etc.

Send an email to info@stephanieobi.com to get started.
If you are more interested in using online courses to reach thousands of entrepreneurs, either as a marketing strategy or as a CSR strategy, my company also runs Trayny, which is an online business school that creates, hosts and manages online courses from Africa's most trusted leaders.

We can partner with your company to train thousands of people irrespective of their location, using online courses.

To find out more about Trayny, please visit www.trayny.com

If you would like to partner with Trayny, send an email to info@trayny.com to get started.

Acknowledgements

I want to start by thanking God for being my Creative Director. Thank You for putting the idea to create an online course in my heart, and sending helpers my way at every step. Thank You for telling me what to write in this book and for giving me the grace to execute.

I want to thank my parents, Mr Sam Obi and Mrs Mayen Obi for giving me the gift of freedom. I can't imagine how I would have felt if my daughter said she wanted to pursue a path I had never heard of, after graduating with a First Class degree in Computer Science. You allowed me to chase my dreams and you support me even to this day.

Thank you for all the sacrifices you made so that I could be exposed to new experiences, attend the best schools and develop my other interests. It is one of those hobbies you supported that led me on this journey. Thank you for bringing me up in the way of the Lord, and for making our house a happy home. I feel so lucky to be your daughter.

I want to thank my siblings:
Thank you Genevieve Obi for caring for me all the time.
Thank you Princess Obi for always being a voice of reason.
Thank you Samuel Obi for helping me with my videos and images.
The three of you are gifts from God to me.

I want to thank my aunt, Aunty Eneanwan for being a second mother to me. Thank you for helping me to get over my fear of mathematics. If I was still afraid of math, I probably would have also been scared of technology and any other thing that seemed complicated.

I want to thank my mentor, Mrs Tara Fela-Durotoye for showing me the power of speedy execution, focus and vision. Thank you for showing me that it's okay to be a pioneer and to trust my intuition. Thank you for teaching me how to pray for my business.

I want to thank my Fathers in the Lord, Bishop David Oyedepo and Pastor Poju Oyemade.

Bishop David Oyedepo, thank you for setting me on the right path. I started listening to you when I was a teenager and since then, your messages have helped me to develop a personal relationship with God. During my time at Covenant University, you made me to realise that I was here to impact the world and at such a young age, you equipped me for the work I am doing now.

Thank you Pastor Poju Oyemade of Covenant Christian Centre for allowing God speak through you to me every Sunday. Your messages have helped me during the most trying seasons of my life and have helped me to live a life of faith.

I want to thank my coaches who have helped me in different phases of my life:

Thank you Bankole Williams for helping me to get rid of the mindset blocks that held me bound for so long.
Thank you Victor Bassey for helping me to find clarity.
Thank you Carla Holden for helping me remember how amazing I am when I lost my confidence.
Thank you Steve Harris for always being available to help and for giving me a book that helped me to find clarity.
Thank you Paul Foh for energising me. Anytime I speak to you, I feel like I can conquer the world.
Thank you Innocent Usar for helping me to become a more compassionate person.
Thank you Annick Ina for spending some time with me to review the outline of this book.
Thank you Sharon Adaigbe for helping me with my book title and with the editing.
Thank you Adeleke Aladekoba for designing my book so thoughtfully.
Thank you Catherine Egwali and Temi Ashabi Ajibewa for helping me to figure out Amazon and for coming to my rescue when I had issues with my manuscript.
Thank you Omilola Oshikoya and Arese Ugwu for inspiring me with your books and giving me tips at different stages of the journey.

I want to thank Ibukun Awosika, Fela Durotoye, Leke Alder, Lanre Olusola and Udo Okonjo for their live sessions, books and audio materials. I listened to these materials continuously and they have opened my mind and taught me secrets I had never seen anywhere else.

I also want to thank a few of my friends who have played defining roles in my business journey:
Thank you Akaoma Onyenoro for being my prayer partner.
Thank you Adura Mokuolu for encouraging me to get serious about my accessories business when I still considered it as a hobby.

Thank you Wunmi Olufeko for acting as a sounding board throughout the years.

Thank you Kemi Onabanjo, Esiri Okotie and David Rufai for supporting me when I started my online course journey

Thank you Remi Owadokun for harassing me to write this book and threatening my life.

Thank you Glory Edozien and Tomie Balogun for being sounding boards and pillars of support.

Thank you Tobi Olanihun for helping me to plan a major event that was key to my online course journey.

Thank you Chichi Eruchalu for being so open with me and encouraging me to get out of my comfort zone. Your friendship is a gift.

Thank you Jide Olatunbode for giving me a home to write the first 10,000 words of my book.

I want to say thank you to my SoConnected family, my Lagos Business School family, my Covenant University family and my TFD Series family. I've learnt so much from being a part of your network and you've made me smile on so many days.

I want to thank Women in Management, Business and Public Service for awarding me with the First Prize in the WIMBIZ Impact Impact Investment Competition in 2014. When I won that prize, it validated my online course idea and encouraged me to go further.

I want to say thank you to Olorisupergal.com for sharing my work on your platform. I remain eternally grateful.

I want to say thank you to the three ladies who have worked with me - Grace Yarmirama, Oriyomi Adebare and Oluwatosin Adedoyin. Thank you for being destiny helpers. I don't know what I would have done without you.

I want to thank my book launch team for helping to spread the word about this book.

To my online community: Thank you for cheering me on, reading my mails, liking my posts, commenting on them, giving me ideas and feedback. I love you from the bottom of my heart. Finally, to everyone who has ever paid for my products: Thank you for believing in me and allowing me to be a part of your success story.

About the Author

Popularly referred to Africa's Queen of Online Courses, Stephanie Obi has launched twenty online courses, across multiple niches and has enrolled over 600 participants from nine countries into her programs.

Given her renowned expertise, she now helps other people to create, launch and sell their own online courses. She is also the founder of Trayny, an online educational platform that creates and manages online courses from Africa's most trusted leaders.

She is a First Class graduate of Computer Science from Covenant University and holds an MBA from the prestigious Lagos Business School. She has received many notable awards and recognitions such as being named as one of the 100 Most Inspiring Women in Nigeria in 2017 and winning first prize in the Wimbiz Impact Investment Competition in 2014.

She speaks in notable conferences around the world and has been featured on various platforms including Channels TV, Guardian Newspaper, Arise TV, Punch Newspaper, EbonyLifeTV, etc.

She shares business lessons weekly on www.stephanieobi.com

I'd love to hear about how this book has helped you.
Please leave a review on Amazon or you can share it on Instagram and tag me @stephobi

Made in the USA
Middletown, DE
12 September 2018